200 YEARS

of

CLYDE PADDLE STEAMERS

ALISTAIR DEAYTON & IAIN QUINN

AMBERLEY

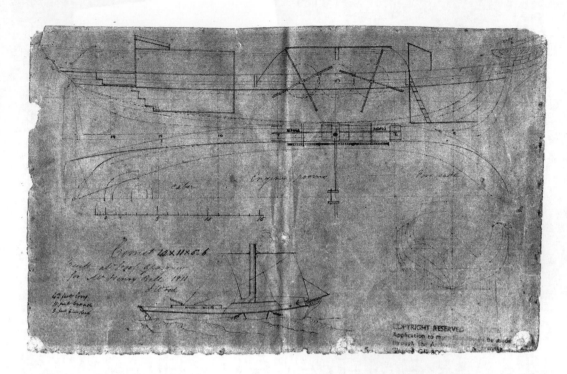

A drawing of the lines of the 1812 *Comet* by John Wood, dated 1833 on the back and given to Robert Napier, now in Glasgow University Archives.

First published 2012

Amberley Publishing
The Hill, Stroud
Gloucestershire, GL5 4EP

www.amberley-books.com

British Library Cataloguing in Publication Data.
A catalogue record for this book is available from the British Library.

ISBN 978 1 4456 0255 4

Typeset in 10pt on 12pt Sabon.
Typesetting and Origination by Amberley Publishing.
Printed in the UK.

Contents

Introduction

This is the story of the Clyde and West Highland paddle steamer over the 200 years since 1812, when Henry Bell's *Comet* operated the first commercial steamboat service in Europe from Glasgow to Greenock and Helensburgh. It tells the story of the development of such ships from the very basic design of the early steamers, little more than powered sailing boats, to the luxury of late nineteenth-century beauties such as *Columba* The steamer services developed from essential transport links to coastal towns, in the era prior to the railway reaching such towns, to excursion services to satisfy the demand for leisure by the industrialised masses brought to the Greater Glasgow area by the industrial revolution and paid holidays for the working man.

In the next 10 years almost fifty paddle steamers were built for use on the Clyde, and by 1841, when a railway opened from Glasgow to Greenock, 160 had been built.

The story includes the sale of the vast majority of the fleet for use in attempting to break the blockade of the Confederate ports during the US Civil War in the early 1860s, the 'Sunday Breakers', steamers used as what were basically floating shebeens, which offended both the church-going majority who would not have dreamed of using public transport on a Sunday and temperance campaigners, of mid-Victorian tales of steamers racing for the piers, and of a handful of shipwrecks, although only a handful with major loss of life.

The towns and villages on the Firth of Clyde developed because of steamer connections with Glasgow, with the rich merchants of that metropolis building their summer homes at such places as Dunoon, Rothesay, and the villages on the Holy Loch, commuting daily or weekly to the city.

Unusually, the reciprocating-engined screw steamer never took on in the Firth of Clyde, apart from the Campbeltown steamers. In 1901 the world's first turbine screw steamer, *King Edward*, entered service and over the next few decades turbine steamers took over most of the longer-distance routes.

In the latter years of the nineteenth century the three railway companies in the area built up fleets of steamers, driving out almost all the private owners and developing an extensive and long-lasting network of routes based on the railheads of Craigendoran, Greenock Princes Pier, Gourock, Wemyss Bay and Fairlie. Both world wars saw the use of Clyde paddle steamers, mainly as minesweepers, with the loss of a number to enemy action and the use of several in evacuating troops from Dunkirk in May 1940.

In addition to Clyde paddle steamers, this book also deals with those which ran to Stranraer, those of the West Highlands, many of which also saw service on the Clyde, and those on Loch Lomond.

The increased use of the motor car and road improvements during the second half of the twentieth century led to a retrenchment of steamer services on the Clyde with short-distance car ferry services replacing many longer distance services. By the 1960s only four paddlers remained in service and after the withdrawal of *Jeanie Deans* in 1964, *Talisman* in 1966 and *Caledonia* in 1969, *Waverley* remained the sole survivor. When Caledonian MacBrayne withdrew her after the 1973 season, an era appeared to be at an end. Sold to the Paddle Steamer Preservation Society for £1, it was thought by many that a future as a static exhibit beckoned but she returned to service in 1975 on the Clyde and has since sailed from many locations round the coast of the UK and is a remarkable survivor continuing in service to this day.

Various engines and parts of engines from Clyde steamers survive in museums and interest is maintained by the Clyde River Steamer Club, celebrating its 80th anniversary in 2012.

Preface

In August 1812 the curious little *Comet* splashed her way from Port Glasgow to the Broomielaw – and then back downriver again to Greenock – at a stately five miles an hour. It was the very first commercial steamship in the world; just one huge cultural legacy was the possibility (for the first time) of transport to a timetable; and, save for the sad grey summer of 1974, paddlewheels have pounded the great waters of the Clyde every summer since.

Henry Bell – inept, pompous, something of an ocean-going balloon and who in many respects epitomised that wry American saying, 'Behind every successful man is an astonished woman,' – is one of those historic characters it is easier to love than to like. Though he had vision and passion, his lofty disdain for detail and great clumsiness with his hands were not the stuff of a great inventor. He could not even settle on a dull, study trade. When he returned to Scotland in 1790, after some vague work in London, it was as a house-carpenter in Glasgow, and not a very good one. He had ambitions to become a civil engineer, and joined the city's Corporation of Wrights in 1797, but got nowhere: he had neither the capital, the skill nor the charm. A bewildered contemporary would conclude that Bell

> had many of the features of the enthusiastic projector; never calculated means to ends, or looked much farther than the first stages or movements of any scheme. His mind was a chaos of extraordinary projects, the most of which, from his want of accurate scientific calculation, he never could carry into practice. Owing to an imperfection in even his mechanical skill, he scarcely ever made one part of a model suit the rest, so that many designs, after a great deal of pains and expense, were successively abandoned. He was, in short, the hero of a thousand blunders and one success.

And even that was scarcely unalloyed. As launched on service, the *Comet* had a pair of spindly paddle-wheels on each side – no doubt by the logic that a horse with four legs is faster than a man with two – driven, with all its limited might, by a 3-horsepower engine. This entirely new sort of ship was for weeks gleefully, Scottishly distrusted as a potentially lethal innovation. William Orr, then a young lad of the town and later a redoubtable Clyde skipper himself, recalled decades later the early arrivals of this smoking, wheezy new sort of boat. 'When she would be reported coming round Baillie Gammell's point, all of us children ran down the quay to see her blow up and see the sailors and passengers "fleein' in the air." We were not much disappointed at the time, as it was sure to happen soon ...' Other operators, of far superior business nous, fast stole his concept, built and launched their own steamers, and made soon away with Bell's trade on the Firth. Resorting to the West Highland wilds, in December 1820 (Bell, with characteristic good fortune, was himself aboard) the wee pioneer was decisively wrecked as she voyaged south from Fort William; all scrambled to safety, as her stern bobbed remorselessly away to the maws of Corryvreckan and was never seen again.

Yet many were (and are) the *Comet*'s children; and on the Firth of Clyde, especially, the paddlesteamer would dominate passenger shipping till far into the twentieth century. They were still being launched in number even in the 1930s; two more appeared after the Second World War; and it would be 1953 before the last major Clyde operator, the Caledonian Steam Packet Co. Ltd (then in the drab, drear guise of the British Transport Commission) ordered its first major vessels with internal combustion engines. Only fourteen years later, though, G. E. Langmuir would gloomily note in a new edition of *West Highland Steamers* that 'it is most unlikely' any new paddlesteamers would be built. The new economies of fuel – and such brilliant innovation as, for instance, Voith-Schneider propulsion – had seen them off.

In an age so smug in its own technology, we forget the genuine advantages paddlesteamers once afforded. With their broad sponsons, they had a certain stately stability and were readily adapted for ferry service. They could accelerate (and stop) with striking speed and their shallow draft allowed them to venture in certain waters (such as those by Craigendoran) where large screw ships could not. And on the Clyde, in particular – and well within living memory – they sustained a new, rich maritime culture: one of rivalry, races, derring-do, all sorts of quiet skulduggery against rivals, dashing masters and prickly engineers and softly spoken crew, many native Gaelic speakers from the Hebrides. They begot, besides, new skills, now largely lost. (In all the Clyde, only one dry-dock facility now survives.)

They were more than ships. Many – the third *Iona*, the venerable *Glencoe*, the great *Columba* and the sturdy *Lucy Ashton* come at once to mind – attained majestic old age. Others, like the ill-fated *Jupiter* of 1937, had curiously brief lives; or spent much of their Clyde course wracked by excessively cutting-edge and unreliable machinery, the 'clockwork mouse' of the *Talisman*, our first (and last) diesel-electric paddler being a case in point. Not a few were lost in the terrible world wars. (On the evening after my very first cruise on the *Waverley*, in 1977, a gracious minister from Lewis quietly told how, staring helplessly from his own craft at Dunkirk, he had watched her 1899 namesake die.) All – even those less than successful, such as the coal-devouring *Glen Sannox* or the wee, forlorn and very slow *Marchioness of Lorne* – established themselves, in their own way, as characters. Decades after they were reduced, by hammer and chisel and the oxy-acetylene torch, to so much cutlery, some to this day have their own passionate following. (Though I never knew her, I have long been seduced by the glamour of the late, great *Jeanie Deans*.)

Had not a few enthusiastic, young and rather tweedy men, nearly forty years ago now, vested their faith in a tired, tatty *Waverley*, not just to preserve her but (against mockery, difficulties, and some surprisingly nasty attacks from within the steamer-dreamer fraternity itself) to keep her sailing, few today under fifty would know anything of the joys of a sea-going paddler in full cry: the moan of a Weir's feed-pump, the deep *chonk* of the low-pressure cylinder; the intoxicating aroma of steam and hot oil; the steady pound, eight-beats-to-the-bar, of those battering floats of American elm ...

But they did, and she lives on. For the others, they voyage yet in the sunlit flood-tide evenings of many a Scottish heart; and, now, once more, in the pages of this book, where Alistair Deayton and Iain Quinn do them honour.

John MacLeod,
Isle of Lewis,
March 2012.

Acknowledgements

The authors acknowledge Ian Millar and Edward Quinn for the use of photographs and Captain Murray Paterson for use of two photographs of the 1962 *Comet*.

The Wotherspoon and Langmuir collections at the Mitchell Library have provided photographs as has the Clyde River Steamer Club, to whom our gratitude is expressed. Both authors acknowledge the many photographers, too numerous to mention, who have freely given use of their photographs, many being published here for the first time.

The records of the late Donald Robertson have been used extensively. During his lifetime Donald sailed on eighty-nine paddle steamers and knew many of the steamers in this volume well. His detail on the subject was superb and has been an invaluable original source of reference. Donald was a founder member of the Clyde River Steamer Club, a man held in high regard and a great influence on many enthusiasts. He served as President and Honorary President of the Clyde River Steamer Club and was Head Office Manager of the Clydesdale Bank. He died in 2003.

Much use has been made of some of the classic volumes on Clyde steamer history: Captain James Williamson's *The Clyde Passenger Steamer, its Rise and Progress during the Nineteenth Century From the 'Comet' of 1812 to the 'King Edward' of 1901*; Andrew McQueen's *Echoes of Old Clyde Paddle Wheels* and *Clyde River Steamers of the Past 50 Years*; Alan Paterson's very detailed *Victorian Summer of the Clyde Steamers* and *Golden Years of the Clyde Steamers* and, to a lesser extent, other books mentioned in the Bibliography.

PART 1

THE HISTORY AND DEVELOPMENT OF THE CLYDE PADDLE STEAMER

Early Steamers and the Development of the Route Network

In August 1812, when Henry Bell's first *Comet* entered service on the Clyde, she ran from Glasgow to Greenock on Tuesdays, Thursdays and Saturdays, a route extended to Helensburgh on Saturdays. She returned on Mondays from Helensburgh and Greenock and on Wednesdays and Fridays from Greenock. On the days she did not serve Helensburgh, a sailing vessel provided the connection from Greenock.

The second Clyde steamer, *Elizabeth*, commenced operations from Glasgow to Greenock and Helensburgh in March 1813, but in April of that year her destination was changed to Gourock, on which route she was joined by *Clyde* later that year when each of the two steamers made a return run from Glasgow to Gourock daily. *Glasgow* of 1813 was the first steamer running from Glasgow to Largs. A further seven steamers were built by the end of 1814 for the Glasgow to Greenock service, also the first *Inverary Castle* for the Glasgow to Inveraray service. *Defiance* of 1817 was the first steamer on the Lochgoilhead service. Inveraray, then spelt Inverary, was an important destination at that time and the route to Lochgoilhead was part of a through route to Inveraray, continuing by horse-drawn coach through Hell's Glen to St Catherine's, and ferry across to Inveraray.

Britannia of 1815 commenced a fortnightly service to Rothesay and Campbeltown, followed by *Waterloo* in the following year. *Dumbarton Castle* of 1815 was the first steamer regularly running to Rothesay, followed in the following year by the first *Rothesay Castle*.

Albion of 1816 was the first steamer regularly serving Millport, also extending her sailings to Ardrossan and Irvine. She was a very slow steamer and Williamson notes that 'the boys of Largs and Skelmorlie were often wont … to run her races.'

The service to Dumbarton was commenced in 1817 by *Duke of Wellington* although the Greenock steamers would have called at Dumbarton prior to that date.

The pioneer cross-channel steamer *Rob Roy* also operated a Glasgow to Arrochar service in 1818 although Arrochar was served by the Loch Goil steamers on certain sailings.

1818 also saw the first steamer on Loch Lomond, *Marion*, and this was also advertised as part of a route to Inveraray, with coaches running from Tarbert over Rest and be Thankful to Loch Fyne.

Robert Bruce of 1819 was the first steamer on the Holy Loch service to Kilmun. The villages around the Holy Loch, and in many other places on the Clyde Coast, developed at this time with rich Glasgow merchants building villas there, many of which survive to this day. This was a pattern which was replicated in other places, with the families relocating to the Coast for the summer and the menfolk commuting to the city daily apart from during the Glasgow Fair fortnight.

In 1912 the *Comet* Centenary celebrations included a decorated tram in Glasgow, as seen here.

The early Clyde paddle steamer and its builder are celebrated in this mural at Exhibition Centre station.

In 1827 David Napier purchased land on the Holy Loch at Kilmun, built a pier there, and a road to the foot of Loch Eck, and in the following year placed the steamer *Aglaia* on Loch Eck with a connecting steam carriage from Kilmun to Loch Eck. A horse coach ran from the top of Loch Eck to Strachur which connected with the steamer *Cupid* to Inveraray. The steam carriage proved too heavy for the road and was soon replaced by a horse coach, but this alternative route to Inveraray enabled the circular route latterly known as 'The famed Loch Eck Tour' to be operated.

A steamer service along the Forth & Clyde Canal was commenced in 1829 with *Cyclops*, and was extended to Alloa on the River Forth.

Marion was the first steamer to go upstream from the city, when she sailed to the Clyde Iron Works at Dalmarnock in 1817, the year before she went to Loch Lomond. The only regular scheduled services upstream from Glasgow were from Hutchesontown Bridge, upstream on the weir in the Clyde, to Rutherglen with Seath's *Artizan*, *Royal Burgh* and *Royal Reefer* which ran between 1856 and 1859 in successive years, each steamer being sold when less than two years old.

The Broomielaw was the departure point for Clyde steamers trips prior to the opening of the railways to the coast railheads. Here can be seen the basic paddle housings that were used before the landing platforms on top of them were introduced. Captain McLean's *Marquis of Bute* is lying of the berth with the bow of the Dunoon & Rothesay Carriers' *Dunoon Castle* in the right foreground; *Petrel*, then owned by H. Dore and on a service to Largs, Millport and Arran, is inboard of her; and Peter Denny's *Loch Lomond* on the Dumbarton Service is to the right of *Marquis of Bute*'s funnel. This picture must have been taken in 1868, as *Loch Lomond* was laid up after that season.

The Broomielaw saw large crowds waiting to embark on the steamers, as seen in this view with the Loch Goil steamer *Carrick Castle* having just departed and Captain Bob Campbell's *Benmore* with the familiar Campbell white funnel at the berth. This was taken between the introduction of *Benmore* in 1876 and the sale of *Carrick Castle* to Leith owners in 1881.

The crowds are evident on the decks of the steamers and on land in this view from 1885 with Bob Campbell's *Benmore* awaiting loading, his *Meg Merrilies*, still with two funnels prior to her reboilering in 1888, in mid-stream, and the bow of the Arrochar steamer *Chancellor* of 1880, Buchanan's 1864 *Eagle* and his recently-purchased *Vivid*, all already with heavy passenger loads and still moored at the quay.

West Highland Services

The first steamer service to Fort William via the Crinan Canal was operated in September 1812 by *Comet* in her inaugural season, and in 1819 she inaugurated a regular service on this route. *Stirling Castle* inaugurated a service on Loch Ness from Inverness to Fort Augustus in 1820, extended to Banavie when the Caledonian Canal was opened on 27 October 1822, when she took part in the opening ceremony and was joined by the second Comet for the section from Loch Oich to Banavie. Two years later she commenced a Glasgow to Inverness service.

Maid of Islay ran the first recorded service to Islay and to Skye in 1825. This was from West Loch Tarbert, with sailings on Tuesdays to Port Askaig, and on Thursdays to Oban, Tobermory, Isleornsay and Portree. The first service to Stornoway from Glasgow was in 1822 by *Argyle* of 1815, which also operated the first sailings from Oban to Staffa and Iona in the following year.

The Broomielaw between 1912 and 1914 with Buchanan's *Isle of Arran* berthing and the Firth of Clyde Steam Packet Co.'s *Ivanhoe* having just departed for Rothesay.

Hull Design

The early Clyde paddle steamers had similar hulls to contemporary coastal sailing ships. Wood was used for the hulls exclusively until 1831 and for certain steamers until the mid-1840s with *Prince* of 1846 being the last conventional Clyde steamer with a wooden hull, although the tug/tender *Flying Scud* of 1866 and the paddle yacht *Comet* of 1892 were both wooden-hulled.

The hull shape of the early steamers had been basic and a list of steamers built by John Wood at Port Glasgow notes that *Robert Burns* (1819) 'was the first boat that was made sharp at the bows' and about *Caledonia* (1815) it states 'This boat was built quite flat to draw little water, having no round in the bottom, something in the form of a chest but sharp at the bows, she was a slow sailor ...'. *Argyle* (1816) and *Lord Nelson* (1816) were similar, but both 'afterwards got a round bottom', although *Argyle* was 'blunt at the bow'.

It has often been claimed that the first iron-hulled steamer was David Napier's *Aglaia* of 1828 on Loch Eck, but she had an iron bottom to the hull and wooden sides. The first iron-hulled steamer on the Clyde was *Fairy Queen* of 1831, although *Cyclops* of 1825 on the Forth & Clyde Canal had an iron hull, as had *Lord Dundas* and *Manchester* of 1831, both also on the Forth & Clyde Canal. *Cyclops* was built as a non-powered craft, with the engine installed in 1829, and was similar to *Vulcan* of 1819, which was iron-hulled but unpowered. The twin-hulled *Lord Dundas* was claimed to be the first iron-hulled steamer to sail on the open sea when she made her delivery voyage from Manchester to Bowling, although that honour belongs to the first-ever iron steamship, *Aaron Manby*, which made her delivery voyage from London to Paris in 1822.

Windsor Castle of 1859 was the first Clyde paddle steamer built of steel, but she had a short career, being sold for use at Calcutta in the following year. She went out under sail, without her engines, and was wrecked on the island of Sanda on her delivery voyage. It was not until *Columba* in 1878 that the next Clyde steamer with a steel hull was built, followed by *Chancellor* in 1880. By the mid-1880s all steamers were being built with steel hulls. *Meg Merrilies* of 1883 was the last Clyde paddle steamer with an iron hull, although *Jeanie Deans* of 1884, *Diana Vernon* of 1885 and *Fusilier* of 1888 had iron and steel hulls.

Comet and other very early steamers were steered by a man at a tiller in the stern but the ship's wheel made an early appearance, controlling the rudder by a system of chains until the advent of the steam steering engine in the 1870s. Steamers were steered from a plank across the paddle boxes that became known as the bridge, hence the modern term 'bridge' for the location from where a ship is commanded. The bridge was open until 1948 when, at the instigation of the National Union of Railwaymen, wheelhouses were added to all Clyde paddle steamers. In the nineteenth century the bridge was generally situated aft of the funnel.

The Deck Saloon

Elizabeth, the second steamer to be built for Clyde service in 1812, was described by Andrew McQueen in *Echoes of Old Clyde Paddle Wheels* as 'having an aft saloon 21 feet long, handsomely carpeted, with seating all around and a sofa across one end. There were six small windows each side, made to slide up and down and thus admit plenty of light and air. Each of them was furnished with tasselled fringes and velvet cornices with gold ornaments, giving a very rich effect. A large mirror and a shelf of 'best-sellers' were also there for the benefit of passengers.'

Most early paddle steamers, though, had small, ill-ventilated cabins with plain wood benches below the main deck fore and aft of the machinery spaces. Bearing in mind the low level of personal hygiene of the working population in that era, with baths being taken infrequently, and illumination by candles or oil lights, they would not have been pleasant places in which to pass the time during the voyage, especially on a rainy day when the mass of passengers would be sheltering down below. There would have been little to see through the portholes, and larger windows would have been in danger of being breached in stormy weather.

In 1853 a solution of sorts was provided in Hutcheson's first *Chevalier*, which had a raised quarter deck, which raised the aft saloon by a few feet, and provided full-size windows on that saloon. This design was known as a half-saloon in Europe, and a couple of examples can still be seen there in *Concordia* on Lake Como and the dieselised *Ludwig Fessler* on the Chiemsee in Bavaria. A further nineteen such steamers (*Mail* of 1860, the Glasgow and Stranraer steamer *Briton*, *Eagle* of 1864, which uniquely had an aft deck saloon fitted above her raised quarter-deck in 1887, *Leven*, *Lennox*, *Ardencaple*, *Rosneath*, *Levan*, *Ardgowan*, *Elaine*, *Lancelot*, *Guinevere*, *Craigrownie*, *Gareloch*, *Viceroy*, *Benmore*, *Sheila*, *Glen Rosa* of 1877, and *Brodick Castle*) saw service on the Clyde.

1857 saw the first deck saloons fitted on a Clyde steamer on *Spunkie* and her sister *Kelpie*, and on the twin-hulled experimental steamer *Alliance*. In the following year *Prince of Wales* was built for Loch Lomond with a fore saloon only and the short-lived *Windsor Castle* of 1859 and *Fairy* of 1861 both had deck saloons, as had the Loch Lomond steamer *Prince Consort* of 1862 and the second *Iona* of 1863. The latter's saloons were removed when she was sold to run the blockade and were fitted to her successor of the same name, where they survived until her demise in 1936. From then onward the majority of paddle steamers were fitted with deck saloons or had them added when refitted at some point in their life. These early saloons were narrow affairs with alleyways round the outside and lengthwise seating along the outer sides of the saloon. It was not until the advent of *Columba* in 1878 that full-width deck saloons were introduced and some settees placed athwartships, thus enabling small, private, cubicle-like areas to be set up if necessary. These more roomy saloons became the norm during the 1880s with *Chancellor* of 1880 being the final Clyde steamer to be built with alleyways around the saloons, only three years after *Adela*, the last flush-decked Clyde steamer, was built.

From the earliest days of the deck saloon, the tops of these were used as a promenade deck. The Caledonian Steam Packet Co.'s *Duchess of Hamilton* of 1890 had the promenade deck extended to the bow with an open rope-handling area underneath and the Glasgow & South Western Railway's *Glen Sannox* of 1892 had the area below the promenade deck plated in to the bow, a design that became the norm by the end of that decade. *Duchess of Fife* of 1903 was the final Clyde paddle steamer to have the sides of the main deck open at the bow, although the North British kept with the open foredeck on the main deck. *Waverley* and *Marmion* were rebuilt with the promenade deck extended to the bow for war service in the 1914–18 war. This solid bow was retained after the war, although *Marmion* had a stability problem and was altered back to an open foredeck after a short and unsuccessful season in 1920.

The concept of saloons on the promenade deck did not arrive until an observation lounge forward and an aft promenade deck saloon were fitted to *Jeanie Deans* in 1932 and *Waverley* in the following year. These were part of the design of the 1934 twins *Caledonia* and *Mercury* and of subsequent paddle steamers right up to *Maid of the Loch* in 1953.

The promenade deck extended to the bow with the sides open below enabled passengers to go right to the bow while ropes were handled from the deck below, as seen here on *Eagle III* at Bridge Wharf in the 1930s.

The Development of Engine and Boiler Design

The original engine fitted in *Comet*, and made by John Robertson, had been built in 1811, a year before the steamer, although history is silent as to whether it was built for use on land, or speculatively in the hope that somebody would be looking for one to place in a ship. The early Clyde paddle steamer engines were of the side-lever type, with *Comet*'s engine being described as a half side-lever type. *Princess Charlotte* of 1814 had the first two-cylinder engine, while *Britannia* of 1815, *Inverary Castle* of 1820 and *Saint Columb* of 1834 had beam engines, smaller examples of a type used as large stationery engines at mines, normally used for pumping water. *St Mungo* of 1835 has the first steeple engine, a type which had been invented by David Napier in 1832 and straddled the paddle shaft with the cylinders below and the crank at the top.

Fairy Queen of 1831, the first iron-hulled steamer on the Clyde, also had the first oscillating engine while *Waterwitch* of 1843 and the sisters *Cardiff Castle* and *Craignish Castle* of 1844 had the first diagonal engines, the former single cylinder and the latter two two-cylinder examples. By the late 1840s the steeple engine came to be the norm with a handful of steamers being built with oscillating engines and by the 1850s the side-lever engine became obsolete with the last such recorded as having been built in 1857 for the little cargo paddler *Carradale*. A variation was the diagonal oscillating engine, first fitted in 1859 to *Pearl* and used on a number of other paddle steamers up to *Grenadier* in 1886. There were two variants of this, one with the two cylinders driving the paddle shaft at an angle, rather than vertically as in the conventional oscillating machinery which was used in the 1866 NB twins *Meg Merrilies* and *Dandie Dinmont*, and the other, a D. & W. Henderson patent, used in both *Lords of the Isles* and in *Ivanhoe*, with the two cylinders in a V-formation, driving the paddle shaft.

The final steeple-engined steamer to be built for Clyde and West Highland service was Buchanan's *Scotia* in 1880, and the final one surviving in Clyde service *Vivid*, which lasted until 1902 and, in the West Highlands, *Gairlochy*, ex-*Sultan*, on the Caledonian Canal, which was destroyed by fire at Fort Augustus in 1919.

By the 1880s the compound engine had been established elsewhere for some years, but it was not until the advent of *Grenadier* in 1886 that the first steamer was built for Clyde or Western Isles service with such an engine and this was the sole example of a compound oscillating engine. The CSP's *Caledonia* of 1889 had an unusual tandem compound engine, with four cylinders on two shafts, and most steamers from the 1890s onwards had compound engines although the NBSP remained faithful to the simple expansion diagonal engine until the advent of *Waverley* in 1899. Buchanan's *Eagle III* of 1910 was the last Clyde steamer built with a single-cylinder engine. The compound diagonal engine can still be seen today on *Maid of the Loch* on Loch Lomond.

The side-lever engine of Henry Bell's second *Comet* of 1822, built by D. McArthur & Co. at Camlachie, recovered from the salvaged wreck of the steamer and now on display in the Riverside Museum at Glasgow.

The 1825 side-lever engine from the 1814 *Industry*, built by Caird & Co. at Greenock and now in the Riverside Museum, Glasgow.

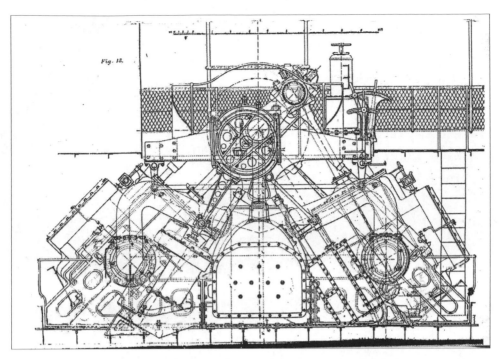

A drawing of the diagonal oscillating engines for the 1877 *Lord of the Isles*, built by D. & W. Henderson, taken from a contemporary copy of *The Engineer* magazine.

A model of the single crank engine of the 1892 *Isle of Arran*, built by W. King & Co. of Glasgow and on display in the Science Museum, London.

The engine room of the 1886 *Madge Wildfire*, built by Hutson & Corbett.

The engine room and compound engines of the 1889 *Galatea*, built by Caird & Co., showing their engine builders plate towards the top of the image.

The engine room of the 1898 *Juno* of the GSWR, built by the Clydebank Shipbuilding & Engineering Co. in the brief period between the demise of J. & G. Thomson and the yard's purchase by John Brown, showing the twin-crank compound engines.

The engine room of the present *Waverley* of 1947, with the triple expansion engines built by Rankin & Blackmore at Greenock.

The CSP introduced triple expansion machinery to the Clyde with *Marchioness of Lorne* in 1891, *Duchess of Montrose* in 1902 and *Duchess of Fife* the following year, although these all had tandem two-crank engines. The first conventional three-crank triple expansion engine built for the Clyde or West Highlands, as seen on *Waverley* today, was *Jeanie Deans* in 1931, although *Culzean Castle*, which had been built in Southampton in 1890 as *Windsor Castle* and came to the Clyde in 1895, and the paddle yacht *Comet* had such machinery.

Coal was the normal source of fuel, although the CSP's *Caledonia* was briefly converted to oil-firing in 1893, and it was not until the 1950s that oil-firing was introduced generally, with *Jeanie Deans*, *Jupiter* and *Waverley* being converted to oil in the winter of 1956/57 and *Caledonia* two years prior to that. *Maid of the Loch* was always oil-fired.

The LNER's *Talisman* of 1935 was the sole Clyde paddle vessel to have diesel-electric machinery, although this proved unreliable and she was on the point of being scrapped when war broke out in 1939. Repairs to the engine enabled her to be of use during the war and following and she was re-engined in 1954.

Boilers

Comet and the early steamers had flue or waggon boilers and it was not until the *Luna* of 1837 that the first tubular boiler was built, although the majority of the steamers from about then had haystack boilers, a primitive form of water-tube boiler shaped like a haystack.

An image of the 1852 *Eagle*, showing the haystack boiler apparently exhausting directly up the funnel.

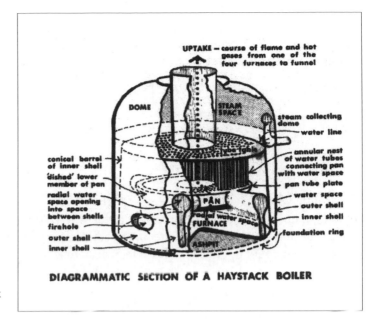

A cutaway drawing of a haystack boiler.

The navy or locomotive-type boiler, a tubular firetube boiler, was used by David MacBrayne in *Iona*, *Columba* and *Grenadier*, although that on the latter was later replaced by a haystack boiler. From 1889 onwards, the introduction of closed stokeholds and forced draughts led to great improvements in performance from the navy boiler. It was used in the GSWR and CSP fleets, while the NBSP and Buchanan kept to the Haystack design.

The Scotch boiler, a variation of the fire-tube boiler where the exhaust gases returned along the upper part of the boiler to a funnel above the firebox, did not really take off on the Clyde, but the double-ended boiler was introduced on *Duchess of Rothesay* in 1895 and the GSWR's *Juno* and *Jupiter* in the following few years and became the standard boiler for Clyde steamers into the twentieth century. Most steamers with two funnels had double-ended boilers, with a flue at each end.

Condensers

Until the late 1870s, most Clyde paddle steamer engines had jet condensers, a design invented by James Watt in 1765 in which a jet of sea-water was pumped into the condensing chamber to help condense the exhaust steam. The drawback of these was that the sea water caused pitting in the boiler. From *Bonnie Doon* in 1876, most steamers were instead fitted with surface condensers, in which the exhaust steam passed through a nest of tubes round which sea water was constantly pumped, thus keeping the boiler water free of impurities. The surface condenser initially got clogged up because of the tallow then used as a lubricant. An early experimental surface condensing system using channels between girders in the hull was fitted by David Napier in *Post Boy* in 1822 but this was only a temporary arrangement and his *Rotary* of 1853 had a self-contained surface condenser.

The Paddle Wheel
by Ian Ramsay

The paddle wheel can trace its ancestry to the undershot water wheel, where the flow of a stream impinging on the buckets or floats of the wheel caused it to rotate and the speed of this water flow and the area of the floats on the wheel being struck developed a rotational power or torque that could be utilised to drive industrial machinery – the earliest use being a mill for grinding cereal into flour. (*See illustration*) The early experimenters who were trying to utilise the steam engine to propel a ship soon saw that the water wheel was capable of being used in reverse for their purpose where, instead of power being developed and available for use at the water wheel shaft, it could be applied there to rotate the wheel. This rotation would cause the floats of the wheel to react against the water in which the ship was floating and cause it to be propelled through the water.

There is always a loss of power in any machine, usually due to friction, but in the paddle wheel there is an added loss due to a phenomenon called slip. A paddle wheel operating in a perfect medium would in one revolution of the wheel cause the ship to move forward by 3.142 x the effective diameter of the wheel across the float centres, as would be found with a pinion gear wheel working on a rack where there would be no lost movement. However, because of slip or the sternward motion imparted to the water by the thrust of the paddle floats acting in what is a yielding medium (water), this sternward motion must be positive, as otherwise the ship would not go forward.

The earliest paddle steamers that operated in open waters had what are called radial paddle wheels, where the floats were fixed to the ends of the radius arms, or spokes, emanating from the hub of the wheel. Because early steam engines ran at very low revolutions, this resulted in large diameter paddle wheels in order to obtain the necessary peripheral travel to get the desired ship speed at the correct float immersion. Float immersion – neither too much nor too little – is very important and this, along with the inherent vulnerability of the paddle wheel to heavy weather damage, led to its early abandonment as a means of propulsion for ocean-going passenger steamers. One of the major problems faced by these ships was the change in immersion of the floats due to the ship's draft decreasing during the voyage as the coal bunkers were depleted by the voracious appetite of the ship's inefficient low-pressure boilers.

This huge coal consumption effectively resulted in paddle propulsion being restricted to cross channel, estuarial and river passenger steamers, where large quantities of coal did not have to be carried for lengthy voyages and where the cargo deadweight in the shape of passengers, mails, cargo and luggage was of light and generally predictable weight. This low cargo deadweight resulted in a fine-lined, easily driven hull which was capable of high speeds and this, along with the improvement in the thermal efficiency of the steam engine and boiler,

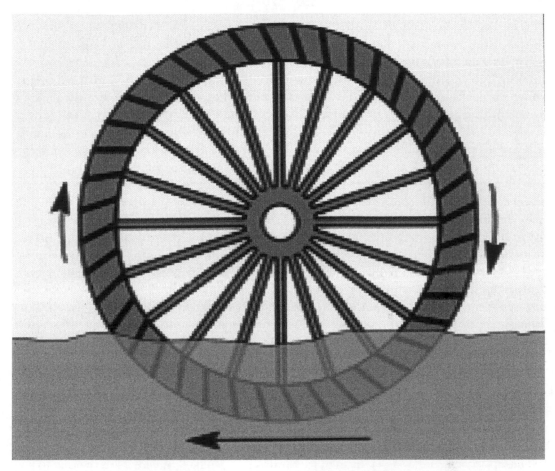

A drawing of an undershot water wheel, a design on which the basic paddle wheel was based.

gave rise to the very-high-speed cross-Channel and excursion paddle steamers of the closing decade of the nineteenth century. Due to the continuing improvement of the propulsion machinery, it was recognised, by the mid-nineteenth century, that the percentage slip of the paddle wheel had to be reduced and various ideas were developed and tried out. The only one that demonstrated a significant improvement was the feathering wheel, which was being simultaneously investigated by several individuals but it is to David Napier, the Clydeside marine engineer, that the greatest credit is usually given.

The radial paddle wheel, which can still be seen on the preserved small paddle steamer *Kingswear Castle*, suffered from a poor float entrance as the water pushed down on entry by each float disturbed the water flow when each float reached its bottom thrust position and the exit from the water was further disturbed by each float trying to lift a volume of dead water. The feathering wheel largely overcame these inefficiencies by causing a float to enter the water in an attitude as near to the vertical as possible, while remaining vertical in the bottom or thrust position and leaving the water in as near vertical an attitude as practicable. This was largely, but never totally, achieved by the introduction of the feathering mechanism.

This required each float to be pivoted at the end of its two supporting paddle arms (the radial spokes again) but restricted in its pivoting movement by radius rods that were pin-jointed at one end to each float's actuating bracket and at the other end to a separate, eccentric-type rotating hub called a 'Jenny Nettle' whose bearing pin was fitted slightly forward of and above the centre of the paddle wheel. On each wheel there was one rod called the king, or driving rod, which was rigidly fixed to the 'Jenny Nettle' rotating hub and which allowed the wheel to exert its full thrust and caused the whole feathering mechanism to operate. A breakage of the driving rod was very serious and resulted in a total failure of the ship's propulsion system. The arrangement of the feathering mechanism must have been arrived at initially by extensive trial and error drawing work, which even in the latter days of paddle wheel design was still required.

By the middle of the nineteenth century there were two types of feathering paddle wheels in use in Britain: (i) the circumferential ring type which protected the paddle floats; and (ii) the Stroudley type which had no outer float protection rings and which can be seen on *Waverley* today. Both types were initially fitted with flat wooden floats but by the end of the nineteenth century the flat floats were being replaced by curved, steel plate floats which were much more efficient and gave a significant increase in speed for the same power or, conversely, the same speed for significantly less power. Like all improvements, it came with a price because a damaged steel float was a heavy and difficult item for the engineers to remove, especially in a seaway, whereas the flat wooden one was made up of several boards and a damaged board could be relatively easily replaced and, indeed, a whole float could be removed if necessary, although with considerable effort and not a little difficulty. It might have been for this reason that the North British Railway and its successor, the London & North Eastern Railway, almost alone, remained faithful to this arrangement and it has proved of considerable benefit to the engineers of *Waverley* during her years of 'preserved' operation.

The advantages and disadvantages of paddle driven ships have already been referred to and its use in sea-going ships finally ended with the development of the efficient screw propeller, but the paddle steamer had one advantage over its screw propelled counterpart and that was its acceleration and stopping power, of great benefit to ferry and excursion steamers making frequent pier calls. Another advantage that the paddle wheel had over the propeller was that it could be fitted in a shallow draft hull while still having sufficient float immersion for high-speed running whereas the same hull, due to the draft limitation, could not accommodate the required diameter of propeller for the same speed. This was a problem that was not solved until *King Edward*'s entry into service in 1901 with her three, small diameter, fast rotating propellers.

Last but not least among paddle driven craft was the ubiquitous paddle tug, which was squat and heavy and had a low free-running speed but with large-area floats that gave good thrust and resultant tow-rope pull. Unlike passenger steamers, many of the tugs had a steam engine driving each paddle wheel, which allowed them to be rotated independently, making them very manoeuvrable and able to pivot on their own axis.

Despite the continued development of the paddle wheel during the nineteenth century – number and spacing of floats, float area, peripheral speed, curved steel floats, etc. – there was no structured scientific approach to the fundamental design of the paddle wheel and these improvements were largely the result of practical experience of problems with ships in service

The paddle wheel of the present *Waverley*, showing the feathering mechanism, a shot taken during her rebuild at Great Yarmouth in 2000 when the outer housing had been removed to enable the wheel to be removed and repaired, to be returned on completion of the overhaul.

The paddle wheel of *Maid of the Loch*, also showing the feathering mechanism, seen from below on the slipway at Balloch during her overhaul.

The paddle box crest from the 1888 *Lucy Ashton*, now on display at the National Railway Museum, York.

gained by individual ship and marine engine builders, all of which was jealously guarded from rivals. It was not until the 1950s that a structured, scientific investigation into the design of the paddle wheel was undertaken by Volpich & Bridge at the Dumbarton Ship Model Testing Tank of William Denny & Brothers. The comprehensive testing programme and subsequent analysis of results bore out the ultimate designs of the paddle wheel (with all the incorporated improvements) although the results were too late to assist in the design of *Maid of the Loch*'s paddle wheels. For anyone who is interested, the complete and very comprehensive results of the investigations can be found in the 1955, 1956 and 1957 *Transactions of the Institution of Engineers & Shipbuilders in Scotland* (IESIS).

Ian Ramsay   © Ian Ramsay 2011

The Expansion of the Railway Network

The early steamers were not excursion steamers, as many of us would remember them, but a vital transport link in the era before railways. Prior to the entry into service of *Comet* in 1812, the only means of transport from Glasgow to Greenock was by coach and horses on very poor roads, or in the flyboats, described by Williamson as 'wherry-built nutshells', taking up to twelve hours for the voyage. McQueen tells us they often ran aground between Renfrew and Dumbarton, and the crew then repaired to the nearest hostelry until the tide rose, leaving the passengers abandoned in the boat.

It was almost thirty years until the railway reached Greenock, with the Glasgow, Paisley & Greenock Railway opening to Greenock in March 1841, thus killing the Glasgow to Greenock steamer trade at a stroke, although the transfer to Custom House Quay, used by the longer distance steamers at Greenock, was by the unsavoury East Quay Lane, where the railway company encouraged men to run rather than walk. The luggage boat service by the Clyde Shipping Co.'s *Glasgow* and *Greenock* continued for another twenty years or so, carrying passengers' luggage for liners sailing from the Tail of the Bank. The railway company chartered a number of steamers in 1841 to run a service from Greenock and formed the Railway Steamboat Co. in the following year. The three steamers *Pilot*, *Pioneer* and *Petrel* were built for them in 1844–45, but in 1847 the company sold all its steamers to G. & J. Burns and the rail-connected sailings were left to the private steamer owners. The Railway Steamboat Co. was revived in 1852 after the Glasgow, Paisley & Greenock Railway had been taken over by the Caledonian Railway in 1851, but only for a couple of years, with the almost all its steamers being sold for use in the Australian Gold Rush.

Dumbarton was not reached until the opening of the Glasgow, Dumbarton & Helensburgh Railway in 1858, and the Dumbarton Steamboat Company continued a service from Glasgow to Dumbarton for three or four years after that, although from July 1850 the Caledonian & Dumbartonshire Junction Railway had been open from Bowling to Dumbarton and Balloch, with connecting steamers operating from the Broomielaw eight times a day.

Helensburgh was also reached by the Glasgow, Dumbarton & Helensburgh Railway in 1858, although it was May 1859 before a connecting boat service to the Gareloch opened. In August 1862 the railway company was taken over by the Edinburgh & Glasgow Railway and in July 1865 by the North British Railway. The following year saw the NB operate steamer services from Helensburgh but the main route, to Ardrishaig, was not successful and only lasted for one summer, although the more local routes for the Gareloch and to Greenock were more successful.

The Wemyss Bay Railway opened from Port Glasgow to the pier station at Wemyss Bay in 1865. Always worked as part of the Caledonian Railway, it was formally taken over in 1893. It operated steamers through a subsidiary company, the Wemyss Bay Steam Packet Co.,

Craigendoran Pier, built in 1882, showing the two arms, with a train in the steamer platform awaiting passengers who are disembarking *Marmion* at low tide up an extremely steep gangplank.

formed in 1864. Initial long-distance services were not successful, and the two steamers built for these routes, *Kyles* and *Bute*, were sold to the Thames after the end of their first season in 1865, although the smaller *Largs* was joined by *Victory* and *Argyle* in 1866 on sailings to Millport and to Rothesay. The company was liquidated in 1869 and sailings from Wemyss Bay were taken over by Gillies and Campbell, owned by the captain of *Largs* and his son-in-law.

1883 saw the opening of a station and pier at Craigendoran, a mile short of Helensburgh, a pier which could be used by larger steamers at all states of the tide. This saw the expansion of sailings by the railway-owned North British Steam Packet Co.

Further down the firth, the Glasgow, Paisley, Kilmarnock & Ayr Railway opened throughout from Glasgow to Ayr in August 1840, although steamer services from Glasgow to Ayr continued with the two *Bonnie Doon*'s and with Bob Campbell's *Waverley* until 1886, and after that as excursion services from Greenock and Gourock right up to the 1960s.

Ardrossan was also reached by rail in 1840, enabling services to Liverpool and Belfast and also to Arran to be operated. It was not until 1882 that this line was continued north to Fairlie Pier, with Largs not reached until 1885, although direct sailings from Glasgow to Largs had ceased some ten years previously with traffic being routed via Wemyss Bay.

The Girvan & Portpatrick Junction Railway was opened in 1870, enabling trains to run from Glasgow to Stranraer, although the line from Dumfries had opened in 1861. The Glasgow & Stranraer Steam Packet Company had been taken over by Langlands in 1864 with *Albion* of 1860 having been the final paddle steamer to operate to a scheduled service to Stranraer, by now from Ayr, until she was succeeded by a screw steamer of the same name in 1865.

Greenock Princes Pier showing the Italianate pier buildings dating from 1894, and *Neptune* berthing.

Gourock Pier, dating from the opening of the railway extension from Greenock in 1889, with *Marchioness of Breadalbane* berthed, showing the magnificent half-timbered pier building which has now been almost completely demolished, with only two or three bays remaining, now finished in grey.

The later years of the nineteenth century saw rival lines being opened to Greenock and to Ardrossan, with the Greenock & Ayrshire Railway opening to Greenock Princes Pier from Elderslie in 1869, being taken over by the Glasgow & South Western Railway in 1872. Princes Pier was one of the most magnificent pier stations of its era, rivalled only by Wemyss Bay. The Glasgow & South Western Railway operated steamers under its own name from Princes Pier, Fairlie and Ardrossan Winton Pier from 1890 onwards, after Parliamentary approval was given for it to do so.

The Lanarkshire & Ayrshire Railway, later to be taken over by the Caledonian Railway, built a line from Cathcart via Neilston and Lugton to Ardrossan Montgomerie Pier, the final part of which opened in June 1890. This enabled the Caledonian and Glasgow & South Western railways to compete on the Arran service. This was, in the end, ruinous to both railway companies and a pooling arrangement was set up in 1908 so that Arran services ran from both Ardrossan piers and the different companies' steamers served the route in alternate years. The service from both piers lasted until the Lanarkshire & Ayrshire route was closed to passengers in 1932 and Montgomerie Pier continued in use for Irish and Isle of Man services until 1965, with a link line having been put in at Stevenston in 1947.

The Caledonian extended its line from Greenock to Gourock in June 1889 by means of a line mainly in tunnel underneath Greenock. This completed the railway network to the coast piers. The company formed a subsidiary, the Caledonian Steam Packet Co. Ltd., to operate steamers and its fleet expanded over the following decade and became the premier Clyde fleet, with the company continuing under LMSR, British Railways and Scottish Transport Group ownership until it merged with David MacBrayne Ltd to form Caledonian MacBrayne in 1973, by which time *Waverley* was its last surviving paddle steamer.

Wemyss Bay was the most magnificent of the railway piers, with the pier and station buildings dating from 1903, and still exists, although now cut back at the seaward end. It is seen here in a postcard view from the early twentieth century with *Marchioness of Breadalbane* berthed at the Millport berth.

Builders and Owners

Comet was built by John Wood at Port Glasgow, who went on to be the pre-eminent builder of wooden-hulled Clyde steamers, building a total of forty Clyde and West Highland steamers over the following 27 years, some on his own and some in partnership with Charles Wood, with James Barclay, with Charles Wood and James Barclay, with J. Horatio Ritchie and, from 1838, by a company known as Wood & Reid.

The first Clyde steamers to be built elsewhere were the luggage boats *Trusty* and *Industry* in 1814, coming from Archibald McLachlan in Dumbarton and the famous yacht-builder Fyfe in Fairlie respectively, the former the first of many steamers built in Dumbarton, the majority of these being built at the yard of William Denny, and the latter the sole steam-powered representative of Fyfe's output.

A. & J. Inglis of Pointhouse, at the mouth of the Kelvin, were expert paddle steamer builders, and built sixteen Clyde paddle steamers between 1864 and 1947, all for the NBR and LNER fleets and Loch Lomond, apart from two twentieth-century examples, *Pioneer* and the third *Mountaineer*, for David MacBrayne. The final two surviving paddle steamers, *Waverley* and *Maid of the Loch*, were built there.

Barclay Curle at Whiteinch built fourteen steamers between 1852 and 1895 for various owners

Barr & McNab of Paisley, later of Renfrew, also built eleven paddle steamers between 1838 and 1855.

Blackwood & Gordon of Paisley, later of Port Glasgow, built eight between 1852 and 1886.

Not all well-known Clyde yards built paddle steamers for service on the River and Firth. Charles Connell & Co., famous as builders of cargo ships between 1861 and 1968, which built 510 ships in that time, was only responsible for a single Clyde paddle steamer, Buchanan's *Eagle* of 1864, although a second, *Mary Anne* of 1863, was laid down but sold on the stocks for blockade running. Fairfield of Govan, one of only three Clyde yards still in existence, now owned by BVT Surface Ships and wholly engaged in naval construction, built six Clyde paddle steamers from *Duchess of Fife* in 1903 to *Juno* and *Jupiter* in 1938, all for the Caledonian Steam Packet Co. Ltd., apart from *Jeanie Deans* for the LNER.

Caird & Co. of Greenock, a major yard of that era, built twenty steamers between 1842 and 1866.

Hunter & Dow of Kelvinhaugh built six steamers in the 1830s.

J. & G. Thomson of Govan and later of Clydebank built seventeen steamers for Clyde or West Highland service from 1852 to 1885 with another one, *Juno*, from the same yard when it

The present *Waverley* under construction at A. & J. Inglis at Pointhouse, at the location of the present Riverside Museum, in 1946, showing the paddle wheel housing and fore deck.

Waverley being fitted out at A. & J. Inglis' yard at Pointhouse in 1947, still to receive her funnels, with DEPV *Talisman* on the slipway for overhaul in the background.

Maid of the Loch being re-assembled on the slipway at Balloch in 1953. She was built at A. & J. Inglis' yard in sections, which were taken to Balloch by train. *Prince Edward* can be seen to the left at Balloch Pier.

became Clydebank Engineering & Shipbuilding Co. Ltd from 1897 to 1899 and a further two, *Duchess of Montrose* and *Mars*, after it was taken over by John Brown's in the latter year.

John Barr of Renfrew, and later Kelvinhaugh, built eight Clyde paddle steamers in the 1840s and 1850s.

J. Henderson & Co. of Renfrew built eight Clyde paddle steamers from 1852 to 1860, with a further four coming after the company had been renamed Henderson, Coulborn & Co. in 1861, but none after it became Lobnitz, Coulborn & Co in 1874, from which time it became famed for building dredgers, which continued until 1964, from 1880 as Lobnitz and latterly as Simons-Lobnitz.

John Reid & Co. of Port Glasgow built eight paddle steamers used on Clyde and West Highland services between 1839 and 1890.

Of the 900 ships built by Scott's of Greenock, only nine saw service on the Clyde and West Highlands, most built in the 1820s and 1830s.

James Lang of Dumbarton, who also operated as Lang & Denny, was responsible for the building of sixteen steamers in the 1820s and 1830s which saw Clyde or West Highland service.

Robert Duncan & Co. of Greenock were one of the few yards on the Clyde to survive the transition from wood to iron shipbuilding and completed twelve paddle steamers for Clyde service from 1832 until Robert Duncan Sr.'s death in 1841. His son, Robert Duncan Jr., built a further seven Clyde steamers at the yard he set up at Port Glasgow in 1862 between 1866 and 1879.

The launch of *Isle of Arran* on 14 May 1892 at T. B. Seath's yard at Rutherglen.

Robert Napier was one of the most prolific of Clyde shipbuilders in the nineteenth century. Of a total of 470 ships built between 1836 and 1900, only six were paddle steamers for use on the Clyde or in the West Highlands, although a good deal more were engined by the firm.

T. B. Seath & Co. of Rutherglen built some twelve paddle steamers for Clyde service between 1855 and 1892, a feat not diminished by their isolated location upriver from the city of Glasgow. The most noted of these was the NB's *Lucy Ashton*, probably more because of her longevity from 1888 to 1949 than because of any advanced design features. Also built there was Buchanan's *Isle of Arran*, in service from 1892 until 1933 on services from Glasgow, and until 1936 on the Thames.

Thomas Wingate & Co. of Springfield, and later Whiteinch, built fourteen Clyde paddle steamers between 1837 and 1867. They were early adopters of the iron hull.

Tod & McGregor built twenty-eight Clyde paddle steamers of a total of 160 ships built between 1835 and 1872 at Mavisbank and later Meadowside.

William Denny of Dumbarton built three steamers along with Archibald McLachlan, and a further twenty-three under his own name and that of Denny Brothers, from 1818 right up to *Caledonia* of 1934. Dennys built, in all, some 1,460 ships between 1818 and 1963.

A number of other builders built five or fewer steamers.

Engine Builders

In the early years, builders like John Wood used third parties to provide engines for their steamers.

These included John Robertson, who built the first engine that was used in *Comet* in 1811, a year before the steamer was built, and built engines for a further five steamers in the ensuing 6 years. Other engineers who built machinery for steamers built elsewhere included:

Boulton & Watt, Soho, Birmingham (three steamers, 1814–19)
James Cook, Tradeston (seven steamers, 1814–25)
Greenhead Foundry, Glasgow (three steamers, 1815–16)
Duncan McArthur & Co., Camlachie (sixteen steamers, 1815–26)
David Napier, Camlachie, later Lancefield (nineteen steamers, 1817–38)
Neilson & Co., Glasgow (four steamers, 1821–46)
Claude Girdwood & Co., Gorbals (four steamers, 1822–35)
Robert Napier & Co., Camlachie, Lancefield and later Govan (forty-two engines, of which six were for ships built by themselves, 1823–61)
T. Wingate & Co., Springfield, later Whiteinch (eighteen engines, of which twelve were for ships which they themselves built, 1832–67)
Murdoch, Aitken & Co., Glasgow (three steamers, 1835–37)
J. & W. Napier, Govan (five steamers, 1836–43)
A. Campbell & Son, Anderston (four steamers, 1852–76)
D. Rowan & Son, Glasgow (four steamers, 1872–92)
Hutson & Corbett, Kelvinhaugh (six steamers, 1885–91)
Rankin & Blackmore, Greenock (twenty-two steamers, 1864–1947, including the present *Waverley*)
W. King & Co., Glasgow (six steamers, 1868–92)

Owners

In the early years of Clyde paddle steamers, some steamers were owned by individuals or partnerships rather than by companies. Some were builder-owners and some captain-owners. The second ever Clyde paddle steamer, *Elizabeth*, was part-owned by John Thomson, builder of her engines, while the fourth, *Glasgow*, had a replacement set of engines built by her owner James Cook in or after 1814.

Many owners only had one ship but the ones we highlight here were those owning several vessels.

The Clyde Shipping Company Ltd was the first company to own Clyde steamers, with the luggage boats *Trusty* and *Industry*, built in 1814 and coming into the company's ownership on its foundation in the following year. The Clyde Shipping Company went on to be one of the major owners of tugs on the Clyde and to operate coastal services from Glasgow to Cork and Waterford. The luggage boats transferred cargo and passengers' luggage from the city of Glasgow to vessels berthed at Greenock and anchored at the Tail of the Bank.

Inverary Castle of 1814 was the first steamer of the fleet that was to become the Castle Steam Packet Company in 1832, each steamer being owned by a separate company prior to that date. The company became the Glasgow Castle Steam Packet Company in 1842 and was taken over by G. & J. Burns in 1846. Their steamers mainly sailed to Rothesay and to Loch

Fyne, and were thus the first on what later became the 'Royal Route' of David MacBrayne from Glasgow to Ardrishaig.

The Dumbarton Steamboat Co. commenced a service from Glasgow to Dumbarton in 1817 with *Duke of Wellington*.

William Young operated steamers on the Clyde, with *Sir William Wallace* and *Robert Bruce* being built for the Glasgow–Largs–Millport–Ayr service in 1838, *Ayrshire Lassie* joining them in the following year, *Lady Brisbane* in 1841, a steamer that sailed on the firth for over 40 years, *Lady Kelburne* in 1843, and *Countess of Eglinton* in 1844.

The Campbeltown & Glasgow Steam Packet Joint Stock Co. Ltd. was founded in 1826 to run *Duke of Lancaster* from Glasgow to Campbeltown, and survived until taken over by Clyde Cargo Steamers Ltd in March 1937, the combined company then being known as the Clyde & Campbeltown Shipping Co. Ltd.

The Lochgoil & Lochlong Steamboat Company was formed in 1825 to run services to Lochgoilhead and did so until it merged in 1909 with the Glasgow & Inveraray Steamboat Company, which was under the same ownership. Its first steamer was the Tay-built *Oscar*, which had been running on the route since 1818, and the two steamers *St Catherine* and *St George*, which were built for it in 1825 and 1826 respectively. The merged company, known as the Lochgoil & Inveraray Steamboat Company Ltd, sold its final two steamers, *Edinburgh Castle* and *Lord of the Isles*, to Turbine Steamers Ltd in 1912 but remained in business as a coach operator until it was wound up in 1941.

James Henderson and Alex McKellar owned a number of steamers on the Helensburgh and Gareloch service from the 1820s until 1865, including *Sovereign* and *George Canning* of 1824, *Sultan* of 1828, *Greenock* of 1830, *Royal Tar* of 1836, *British Queen* in 1837, and others.

David Napier owned a number of steamers in addition to being an engine builder. These included *Caledonia* of 1821, *James Ewing* of 1825, the little *Cupid* of 1828, which ran initially from Strachur to Inveraray, and *Venus* of 1827, *Loch Eck* of 1829, *St Mun* and *Kilmun* of 1831, all of which ran on the Kilmun route after he had purchased land at Kilmun, built a hotel and some villas and opened a pier there in 1827.

Captain Duncan McKellar established himself as the main operator on the route from Glasgow to Largs and Millport, stating with *Hero* in 1832, and continuing up to *Juno* in 1860. In 1844 he joined forces with a Mr D. Allan to form the Largs & Millport Union Steam Boat Company, which became the Largs & Millport United Steam Packet Company by 1852 and reverted to the original name by 1859.

The Bute Steam Packet Co. was formed in 1835 to operate *Isle of Bute* and *Maid of Bute* on the Glasgow to Rothesay service until they were sold seven years later to the Railway Steamboat Company.

The Ardrossan Steamboat Co. introduced a service from Ardrossan to Lamlash in 1837 with *Isle of Arran*, followed by *Earl of Arran* from 1860 to 1868.

In 1842 the Glasgow, Paisley & Greenock Railway founded the Railway Steamboat Co., purchasing *Isle of Bute* and *Maid of Bute* from the Bute Steam Packet Co. and building *Pilot*, and *Pioneer* in 1844 and *Petrel* in 1845 for use on rail-connected services from Greenock but these were all sold in 1847 to G. & J. Burns. In 1852 the railway company, by then the Caledonian Railway, re-formed the Railway Steamboat Company and had three small steamers, *Gourock*, *Helensburgh* and *Dunoon*, built for it but the latter two were sold at the end of that season to owners in Australia, where a gold rush was stimulating demand for steamers, only *Helensburgh* making it to the Antipodes, and *Gourock* was sold in the following year, eventually operating at Riga in Latvia. Other steamers, *Glasgow Citizen*, *Eva* and *Flamingo*, were used in 1853, all three being sold to Australia and only the first making the journey successfully. The Railway Company gave up steamer-owning after 1853, coming to arrangements with various private owners to provide rail-connected services.

In 1853 the Eagle Steamer Co. was formed to purchase the steamer *Eagle*, which had been built in the previous year for various members of the Denny family. This company was owned by Captain William Buchanan, Captain Alexander Williamson senior and John Cook, the first time the names of Williamson and Buchanan featured in Clyde Steamer ownership. They were destined to be the final private owners on the river after the advent of the railway fleets in the 1890s. The Eagle Steamer Company also operated *Petrel* and *Cardiff Castle* in the 1850s. By the end of that decade Williamson and Buchannan were joint owners and in 1862 Williamson sold his share in the company to Captain Buchanan. *Eagle* was sold for blockade running in 1862 and was succeeded by a second steamer of the name. Captain Buchanan took over the Ardrossan to Arran service in 1874 and the steamers of Keith and Campbell in 1885, along with their services from Glasgow to Helensburgh, Kilmun, the Gareloch and Arran. His sons succeeded him and Buchanan Steamers Ltd was founded in 1905. A succession of steamers was built for and purchased by the company, latterly with names beginning with 'Isle of'. In 1919 the company merged with John Williamson & Co. to form Williamson-Buchanan Steamers Ltd, continuing to operate services direct from Glasgow until 1939, the company having been taken over by the Caledonian Steam Packet Co. Ltd in early 1936.

Alexander Williamson senior set up his own fleet from 1862 onwards, what became known as the 'Turkish Fleet' of *Sultan*, *Sultana*, and *Viceroy*. This continued with new steamers with the suffix 'more' from the 1890s onwards, by which time his son John was running the company. His other sons, Alexander junior and James, were Marine Superintendent and Manager/Secretary of the Glasgow & South Western Railway and the Caledonian Steam Packet Co. Ltd steamer fleets respectively, although James was also involved with the original owners of *Ivanhoe*, the Firth of Clyde Steam Packet Co.

James Henderson, who owned a shipyard at Renfrew, had built for his own fleet *Diamond* in 1853, *Gem* and *Ruby* in 1854, and *Pearl* in 1859, and was part-owner of a second *Ruby* in 1860.

In 1854 Captain Bob Campbell of Kilmun and his uncles John and Alex (senior) purchased the steamers *Duchess of Argyle* and *Victoria*, and had *Express* built, followed by other steamers on the Garelochhead and Kilmun routes. By the late 1860s, Captain Bob was in full control and in October 1871 he joined forces with Hugh Keith & Co. to form Keith & Campbell. Keith owned the elderly *Lady Brisbane*, which was renamed *Balmoral*. Keith & Campbell got into financial trouble and sold out to Captain Buchanan in 1884, but Bob Campbell purchased *Meg Merrilies* a few weeks after the deal had been done and placed her on the Kilmun service. At the same time he ordered a new steamer, *Waverley*. By this time his sons, Peter and Alec, were involved in the business. *Madge Wildfire* was built for the Campbells in 1886 and in 1888 both she and *Meg Merrilies* were sold to the Caledonian Railway. Captain Bob Campbell died on 10 April 1888 and was buried at Kilmun, with a funeral procession of a long line of steamers from Glasgow and Greenock to the Holy Loch. *Waverley* had been chartered to Bristol in the summer of 1887 and Peter and Alec moved their business to Bristol in 1889, P. & A. Campbell being notable as excursion steamer operators in the Bristol Channel for the next ninety years.

Captain Duncan Stewart began operating steamboats in 1855 and had built for him over the following years *Alma*, *Argyle*, *Victory*, *Athole* and *Lorne*, and purchased *Undine*. These were mainly for the Rothesay service. He died in 1877 and his sons sold the remaining steamers *Elaine* and *Undine* two years later.

The shipbuilders Tod & McGregor owned the sisters *Spunkie* and *Kelpie* in 1857, the former on the Millport service and the latter on a Kyles of Bute route. They had previously owned *Modern Athens* from 1849 to 1852 on the Islay route and *Invincible* from 1853 to 1857 on the Millport service.

Captain Sandy MacLean purchased *Vulcan* of 1854 in 1864 from James McIntyre and placed her on the Glasgow to Rothesay service. He introduced *Marquis of Bute* in 1868 and purchased *Athole* from Captain Duncan Stewart in 1872, both for the Rothesay route. He retired in 1888, *Marquis of Bute* being sold to Captain Alexander Williamson senior, who sold it on to the Glasgow & South Western Railway in 1891 along with the remainder of his fleet. *Athole* went to the Bute Steam Packet Ltd and on to Captain John Williamson in 1898, although she seems never to have operated for him. *Vulcan* had been sold in 1872 to J. & G. Thomson to ferry their workmen from Govan to the new shipyard at Clydebank.

In 1864, the Wemyss Bay Railway Company set up the Wemyss Bay Steamboat Co. as a separate company, as at that time railways were forbidden to operate steamer services. They had *Largs* built in that year, purchasing *Victory* from Captain Duncan Stewart and building the two large steamers *Kyles* and *Bute* in the following year. They outreached themselves with these and services to Arran and Ardrishaig. The two large steamers were sold after this season and *Argyle* purchased from Captain Stewart at the beginning of the following summer. In 1869 the Wemyss Bay Steamboat Company sold its steamers and routes to Captain James Gilles and his son-in-law Captain Alexander Campbell, who had entered steamer ownership in the previous year by purchasing *Venus* from Duncan McKellar.

Captain Alexander Watson was owner of *Rothesay Castle* and part-owner of *Arran Castle* of 1864, and was lost when the latter foundered en route to the Thames in the spring of 1865. He was associated with Henry Sharp, owner of a string of Sunday breakers (q.v.).

In 1866 the North British Railway set up a steamer-operating subsidiary, the North British Steam Packet Co., and had two large steamers, *Dandie Dinmont* and *Meg Merrilies*, built. A service from Helensburgh to Ardrishaig was no more successful than that of the Wemyss Bay Company in the previous year. Subsequent years saw a contraction to more local service to the Gareloch and Holy Loch until Craigendoran Pier was opened in 1882, after which a whole fleet of steamers was built for the company. In 1902 ownership passed to the railway company, who by then had obtained permission to operate steamers, although not to Campbeltown, the east side of Arran or Loch Fyne, and steamers continued to be built up to *Marmion* in 1906 and *Fair Maid* in 1915, a steamer which never saw service on the Firth and was lost during the First World War. The railway company became part of the London & North Eastern Railway in 1923 and *Jeanie Deans* was built in 1931, the diesel-electric paddler *Talisman* in 1935 and the present *Waverley* in 1947.

In 1865, the Greenock & Helensburgh Steamboat Co. Ltd was formed to operate steamer services between these two towns and on to the Gareloch. The steamer *Nelson* of 1855 was purchased from Henderson & McKellar, and four new small steamers were ordered, *Ardencaple*, *Rosneath*, *Levan* and *Ardgowan*, which entered service in the following year. The service was not a success and all the steamers except *Ardencaple* had been sold by spring 1867, with her going in 1869.

Graham Brymner was manager of the Greenock & Helensburgh company but set out on his own as a shipowner in 1867 when *Elaine* was built for him and placed on the Glasgow to Millport service. She was followed by *Lancelot* in 1868 and *Guinevere* in the following year. *Craigrownie*, a larger sister to the four Greenock & Helensburgh steamers, joined the fleet in 1870 but in October 1871, he sold all his steamers.

Seath & Steele, the Seath of this company being T. B. Seath, owner of the eponymous Rutherglen shipyard, ran an excursion service from Glasgow to Ayr from 1866 until 1880 with the newly built *Vale of Doon* and *Vale of Clwyd*, purchased from owners in Wales, and with two steamers named *Bonnie Doon* of 1870 and 1876 respectively.

Dunoon Castle was built in 1867 for a consortium of Dunoon and Rothesay carriers to provide a better and less expensive freight service than the current steamer owners. Within a few years she was in the hands of the Sunday cruise operators, but redeemed herself when she ran for Hill & Company from Fairlie to Millport as *Arran*, along with *Cumbrae*, ex-*Victory*, from the opening of Fairlie Pier in 1882 until the advent of the GSWR steamers in 1892. Otherwise, Hill & Company operated screw cargo vessels and was one of the predecessors of Clyde Cargo Steamers, formed in 1915.

The Duke of Hamilton's trustees operated the Ardrossan to Arran service from the time that *Earl of Arran* was withdrawn in 1868 until 1874 with *The Lady Mary*, built in the former year, and *Heather Bell*, built in 1871. In 1874 Captain Buchanan took over the service with *Rothesay Castle*.

In 1877 the Loch Goil Company set up a new company, the Glasgow & Inveraray Steamboat Co. Ltd, to operate the new *Lord of the Isles* on a daily return service from Glasgow to Inveraray in partial competition with MacBrayne's *Columba*. A second, improved, *Lord of the Isles* followed in 1891. The company was merged with the Lochgoil Company in 1909 and was taken over by Turbine Steamers Ltd in 1912.

Shearer Bros of Greenock had a brief spell of Clyde steamer ownership from 1877 to 1881 with *Glen Rosa*, initially in competition with Hugh Keith's *Guinevere* and, from June 1880, in co-operation with her.

In December 1888, in anticipation of the opening of the railway to Gourock and the opening of the pier there, the Caledonian Railway formed a subsidiary, the Caledonian Steam Packet Co. Ltd, to operate steamers from Gourock, Wemyss Bay and Ardrossan Montgomerie Pier. The first steamers were *Meg Merrilies* and *Madge Wildfire*, purchased from Peter and Alec Campbell, along with the goodwill of the Glasgow to Kilmun service, which they maintained until 1908. A succession of steamers followed, starting with *Caledonia* in 1889 and continuing to *Duchess of Fife* in 1903. The company continued after the railway grouping of 1923, as part of the London, Midland & Scottish Railway, with a number of paddle steamers being built in the 1930s, the final ones being *Jupiter* and *Juno* in 1937. Railway nationalisation in 1948 saw the Caledonian Steam Packet Co. becoming part of British Railways and changes in 1969 saw it become part of the Scottish Transport Group. In 1973 it became part of Caledonian MacBrayne and, in the following year, that company disposed of its last paddle steamer when *Waverley* was sold to the Paddle Steamer Preservation Society for £1.

In November 1891, Morris Carswell formed The Scottish Excursion Steamer Co. Ltd to operate the paddle steamer *Victoria*, which had been built for Gillies & Campbell in 1886 and had been running out of Belfast on charter since 1890. She operated on the Fairlie to Campbeltown route for two seasons but was damaged by fire while lying at the Broomielaw on 17 September 1896 and was sold to London owners in the following May.

In 1892, the Glasgow & South Western Railway obtained Parliamentary powers to operate its own paddle steamers, although it was not allowed to sail to Lochranza, Campbeltown, or Inveraray, purchasing four from Captain Alexander Williamson senior, and a further one each from the Lochgoil Company (*Chancellor*) and Captain William Buchanan (*Scotia*). Three steamers were built in the following year, *Neptune*, *Mercury* and the magnificent *Glen Sannox*, the latter for the Ardrossan to Arran service. Further steamers followed until *Mars* in 1902. When the railway company was absorbed into the London, Midland & Scottish Railway in 1923, the remaining steamers came under the ownership of the LMSR, some being transferred to the CSP, *Glen Rosa* of 1893 being the final survivor, sailing until 1938.

The Glasgow, Ayrshire & Campbeltown Steamboat Co. Ltd was formed in 1895 to operate the Fairlie to Campbeltown route with the large paddle steamer *Culzean Castle*, purchased from Bournemouth owners, for whom she had run as *Windsor Castle*, but the company only survived for three years.

Andrew Dawson Reid was associated with several short-lived companies around the turn of the century. The Clyde Steamers Ltd operated *Duchess of York*, ex-*Jeanie Deans*, from 1897, and *Victoria* from 1898. In May 1898 a new company, The Glasgow Steamers Ltd, was set up to run *Duchess of York*. In 1900 both companies were wound up and were succeeded by Reid Ltd, running *Duchess of York* in 1902 and 1903. A further company controlled by Dawson Reid was the Isles Steamship Co., which operated *Lady of the Isles*, the former *Lord of the Isles* of 1877, on charter from him in the summers of 1903 and 1904.

Captain Alex Cameron owned The Vale of Clyde Steam Packet Co. Ltd, to operate *Madge Wildfire* in the summer of 1911, and The Lady Rowena Steamship Co., to operate *Lady Rowena* from 1912 to 1914, both on excursions from Glasgow to the coast.

When *Waverley* was donated to the Paddle Steamer preservation Society in 1974, Waverley Steam Navigation Co. Ltd was founded to own her and Waverley Excursions Ltd to operate her from 1978 onwards.

Loch Lomond and West Highland Steamer owners

David Napier owned the first steamer on Loch Lomond, *Marion*, in 1817 and joined forces with a Mr McMurrich in 1829. The original Loch Lomond Steamboat Co. was formed in 1825 to operate *The Lady of the Lake* and was succeeded by another company of the same name in 1828, and by the New Loch Lomond Steamboat Company in 1844, which merged with Napier & McMurrich in the following near to form a third company known as the Lochlomond Steamboat Company which lasted until taken over by the North British Railway in 1888. The Dumbarton & Balloch Joint Line Committee, jointly owned by the North British and Caledonian Railways, took over in 1896, this becoming jointly LNER and LMSR-owned in 1923 until it was nationalised in 1948.

Robert Napier operated a number of steamers on West Highland services, from *Stirling Castle*, which ran initially from Inverness on Loch Ness, in 1820 to *Shandon*, built in 1839, which introduced the red funnel with black top that was later adopted by Hutcheson, and by David MacBrayne.

Ayr of 1825 was the first steamer owned by G. & J. Burns in 1824, later to be associated with the formation of the Cunard Line, and to become part of Burns & Laird Line, famous on the routes from the Clyde to Ireland. She was not a cross-channel steamer but was placed on a route from Glasgow to Ayr and Stranraer. By the mid-1830s they were establishing themselves in the West Highland trade by acquiring the steamers *Inverness* and *Rob Roy* from William Young, and also *Helen McGregor*, which was under construction for Mr Young and *Glen Albyn*, independently owned. They formed the North British Steam Navigation Co. and in 1846 acquired the Glasgow Castles Steam Packet Company. In 1851 they sold the West Highland steamers to David Hutcheson, a condition of the sale being that he continued to employ as clerk their nephew, David MacBrayne, who took the business over in 1879, and whose name has become familiar to all who have sailed in West Highland waters up to the present day with the ferries of Caledonian MacBrayne.

James Matheson, who had purchased the island of Lewis in 1844, was part-owner of *Falcon*, which ran from Ardrossan to Stornoway in 1845, and then had built *Mary Jane* in the following year to run from Glasgow to Stornoway. She was too small for the route, and was replaced in 1848 by *Marquis of Stafford*, which was too big for the trade and only lasted a couple of years on the service. In 1871 he placed the old former Dover to Calais mail steamer *Ondine* (1847) on a route to Ullapool from Stornoway, which she maintained until it was taken over by Hutcheson in 1877 and the mainland terminal moved to the railhead at Strome Ferry.

With one exception, the steamers on the Forth & Clyde Canal were owned and operated by the canal company, who also owned horse-drawn so-called 'Swift' boats on the canal. *Edinburgh* of 1832 was initially owned by the London, Leith, Edinburgh & Glasgow Shipping Co. but was purchased by the canal company after only three months in service.

Liveries

Little is known of the colour schemes of early Clyde steamers but *Comet* had a black funnel, hull and paddle boxes. The few illustrations of such vessels show a similar colour scheme, although some of the wooden hulls were left in the original condition and not painted.

The oft-repeated story is that Robert Napier, when delivering an engine for a steamer, also supplied a funnel, red with a black top and thin black hoops. Such black-topped red funnels were used by G. & J. Burns and by their successors in the West Highland trade, Messrs Hutcheson and David MacBrayne, although the black hoops were painted over from about 1905 when David MacBrayne became a limited company, continuing in an amended form into the present-day funnel colours of Caledonian MacBrayne. The Burns' connection with the founding of the Cunard Line meant that this also became the funnel colour of Cunard steamers.

The Dumbarton Steamboat Company had funnels with almost equal sectors of black, white and black and blue paddle boxes, while the Glasgow Castle Company had two white bands at the top of a black funnel, a colour scheme revived by Shearer Bros & Ritchie for the 1877 *Glen Rosa*.

It was not until the 1860s and 1870s that there was much variety in steamer liveries.

The Lochgoil Company had a red funnel with two thin white bands, separated by a thin black band, below a black top. These colours were also used by the two *Lords of the Isles* and by the McKellar steamers on the Largs and Millport run. The second *Lord of the Isles* was the final Clyde steamer to have a copper waste steam pipe running up the funnel. These had been common in the mid-Victorian era, but were later painted black.

The North British Railway and North British Steam Packet steamers had white paddle boxes and black-topped red funnels until 1883, when the white band was added and the paddle boxes became black.

Williamson and Buchanan both used black paddle boxes and a black funnel with a thin white band below the top until Williamson changed to white paddle boxes in 1896 and a black-topped white funnel in 1898. The Buchanan steamers had white paddle boxes from 1913 onwards. This was used by Williamson-Buchanan Steamers after the merger of the two companies in 1919 and the take-over by the LMS/CSP in 1936, although *Queen Empress* had a CSP funnel in 1938 and 1939, when she worked as part of the CSP fleet on rail-connected services. The black funnel with the white band was also used by Duncan Stewart's steamers on the Rothesay route, which also had white paddle boxes, and by Henry Sharp's Sunday Breakers and, with a narrower white band, by *Dunoon Castle* sailing for Dunoon and Rothesay Carriers. Captain James Williamson's Firth of Clyde Steam Packet Company used a yellow funnel with a thin black top ring on *Ivanhoe*.

The white funnel was used by Captain Bob Campbell of Kilmun and by his sons and their company on the Bristol Channel and can still be seen there in the preserved motor vessel *Balmoral*, while the Wemyss Bay Steamboat Company and their successors, Gillies and Campbell, used a black-topped white funnel, as did Captain Dewar's *Marquis of Lorne*.

Hugh Keith's steamers had red funnels with three narrow white bands, while the steamers of Seath & Steele on the Ayr run had cream funnels.

P. & A. Campbell had a yellow funnel for a while, with blue hulls and pink saloons.

The Arran steamers operated by the Duke of Hamilton's Trustees and those of Graham Brymner and the Greenock & Helensburgh Steamboat Co. had black funnels and green hulls and paddle boxes.

Dawson Reid had a very unusual livery from 1897 to 1899 on *Duchess of York*, ex-*Jeanie Deans* of 1884, with a grey hull and paddle boxes, white saloons and a yellow funnel with two narrow white bands separated by a yellow band towards the top. In 1912 Captain Cameron used a green hull and red funnel with black top on *Madge Wildfire*, which had worn a yellow funnel with black top in 1911, as had *Culzean Castle*. *Ivanhoe*, under the ownership of the Firth of Clyde Steam Packet Co. Ltd from 1911 to 1914, had white funnels, with a thin black top added from 1912.

In general, at this time deck saloons were finished in mahogany or teak. Exceptions were the North British steamers, which were cream until 1883, and brown and cream after that date, and those of Captain Bob Campbell, the Firth of Clyde Steam Packet Co.'s *Ivanhoe*, and Gillies & Campbell's *Victoria*, which were white. Some individual steamers used a pale pastel colour on the deck saloons, including Buchanan's *Scotia*, latterly before her takeover by the GSWR, and *Viceroy*.

The period from the 1890s until 1914 saw the greatest variety of colour schemes on the Firth. To quote Cameron Somerville in *Colour on the Clyde*:

The Caledonian Steam Packet Co. had an attractive colour scheme of green underbody (this was experimental and was later changed to the brown which remained until the end), white boot-toping, giving to a blue-black hull with two gold lines. The exterior decoration of the saloons was intricate but lovely, giving indeed some colour on the Clyde. Commencing downwards from the 6-inch skirting-board at the rail of the promenade deck, there came first a narrow band of pale blue, then all the saloon was pink down to the window framing. (Each window-the glass-in these days was always set in a rolled frame and never in an opening, nakedly cut or punched out of a steel sheet.) The framework of each window was painted in white enamel with a beading of pale blue down the vertical edges. The astragals, or the very narrow uprights between the frames, were then of the main colour – pale pink with a vertical white bar down the middle. The glass of each window was divided vertically down the centre by teak, but the uppermost 1/6th or 1/4th was of little vertical panes of coloured glass, these forming one piece which opened inwards and downwards as a fanlight. Of course the scheme differed from steamer to steamer as there were only three sister ships in the Caley fleet. The windows of all the Clyde boats were large and many, amazingly so, considering the stormy passages that had so often to be made. The dazzling white paddle boxes carried the glorious badge of her name, with the name itself in gold leaf on a pale blue ground. The yellow funnel was done in columite, which, of course you all know.

The steamers of the North British Railway had glossy black hulls with two gold lines all round, white boot-topping, saloons pleasingly pencilled and panelled in two shades of ochre, black paddle boxes with a golden image of the hero or heroine, and much more gold around the edges of vents and name and the red funnel with white band and black top.

Buchanan's boats were all black with white saloons, and black funnel with white band; those of Captain Williamson had a black hull and white paddle boxes, and white funnel with black top, the Campbeltown funnel was black, a broad band of red, and black again; the *Lord of the Isles* and the *Edinburgh Castle* had red funnels with two white bands with black between and a black top; while the prettiest colours of all were those of the Glasgow and South-Western Railway which it is said, took their scheme from an experiment on the old *Viceroy*, and had a red underbody, with pale blue-grey hull, a teak beading around the hull, white saloons, much gold lettering on the handsome [white] paddle boxes and bright red funnels with black tops.

The detail of these colour schemes unfortunately cannot be made out in most black and white photographs from the era.

1914 was saw an end to such extravagance and when services resumed in 1919, the fancy details had vanished in the main, never to return, although the CSP saloons continued as before until 1924, when they were painted white.

The railway amalgamations of 1923 saw the LMS, which had absorbed the Caledonian and Glasgow & South-Western railways, try to merge the two colour schemes, with a yellow funnel with red band and black top. In 1923 the former Glasgow & South Western steamers retained their grey hulls, but all had black hulls in 1924 and in 1925 a yellow funnel with black top was adopted; this survived until the formation of Caledonian MacBrayne in 1973, with the addition of a red lion rampant in 1965.

The LNER, which the North British Railway fleet became part of, continued with the NB funnel colours. In 1936, in an attempt to be 'modern', a colour scheme of grey hulls with white superstructure and deck saloon and grey paddle boxes was introduced, amended in 1939 on *Talisman*, when the area of grey paint on the hull was raised to above the saloon windows.

Wartime, of course, saw dreary colours of yellow ochre and all-over grey, although the funnel colours remained as in peace-time. The resumption of services in 1946 saw the two surviving LNER steamers back to the pre-1936 colours, with the observation saloons and deckhouses in a 'scumbled' wood-effect colour scheme. A similar scheme was applied to *Waverley* in her inaugural season of 1947.

1948 saw the nationalisation of the railways, with all Clyde steamers coming under the CSP banner and receiving black-topped yellow funnels. In 1955 *Talisman*'s paddle boxes were painted white, as were those of *Waverley* from 1959 until 1971. *Waverley*'s deck saloons had been painted white in 1953. In 1965, the CSP fleet received new colours, in line with British Rail's corporate image rebranding. Hulls were painted in 'monastral blue', a colour which varied in photographs depending on the weather conditions and the colour of the sky reflected in the water, and the funnels had a red lion rampant affixed to them. In 1970 the hull colour reverted to black, in 1972 the paddle boxes of *Waverley*, by then the sole surviving paddler, were painted black with a white rim, and in 1973, on the formation of Caledonian

MacBrayne, her funnels were painted in their colour scheme of red with black top and a yellow spot in which sat the lions. Her paddle boxes were black with a white surround in that year.

On entering preservation in 1975, *Waverley* regained her LNER funnel colours and black paddle boxes, and in, 2000, on her rebuild, the 'scumbled' effect on her deckhouses. At various times she has had one or two gold lines around her hull.

On Loch Lomond, grey hulls and pink panelled salons were the norm from the advent of *Waterwitch* in 1844 until 1949, when two surviving steamers, *Prince Edward* and *Princess May*, received black hulls and paddle boxes and white saloons. Funnel colours were black, and occasionally red with a black top, until the North British takeover in 1888, when the NB colours were adopted. From the take-over of services by the Dumbarton & Balloch Joint Line Committee in 1896 to railway nationalisation in 1948, funnels were red with a black top.

On nationalisation, the funnels became yellow with a black top and in 1949 the hulls were painted black. In 1953 and 1954 *Prince Edward*'s funnel was all yellow and her hull was white again, but in May 1953 the funnel received a thin black top and in August of that year a full black top. During *Maid of the Loch*'s re-erection at Balloch, she had a black top to her yellow funnel, but when she entered service she had a plain yellow funnel and throughout her time in service had a white hull and white paddle boxes. For the first few weeks of the 1975 season she had a black top on her yellow funnel, and for the remainder of the season a black-topped red funnel, but reverted to the all-yellow funnel in 1976. While she was laid up at Balloch during the 1990s, PSPS members painted her in her current colour scheme of black hull and paddle box and red black-topped funnel, although she has never sailed yet under these colours apart from the short tow across to the slipway to test the rebuilt steam slipway engine in 2008.

Racing

In the days of the private owners, the early and mid-Victorian era before the railway companies took up steamer owning, racing was a common practice as captains vied to see who had the fastest steamer and could get to various piers first.

In August 1827 the Northern Yacht Club, now the Rhu-based Royal Northern and Clyde Yacht Club, organised a steamer race from Rothesay Bay to off Cumbrae and back. This was won by *Clarence*, with *Helensburgh* coming second. These continued for a few years.

On 24 July 1835, *Earl Grey*, while preparing for a race with *Clarence*, suffered a boiler explosion while lying at Greenock. There were six fatalities and about twenty people were injured.

The opening of the railway to Greenock in 1841 led to an outbreak of racing between rival steamers for Rothesay or Largs. The public formed what was loosely termed the Clyde Steamboat Racing Ring and results were generally made known, with different people having their favourites.

Another period of racing started in 1854, when *Rothesay Castle* and *Ruby* were built for different owners for the Glasgow to Rothesay route. Both were sold off the river in 1860, and in the following year a new *Rothesay Castle* and *Ruby*, along with *Neptune*, all built in that year for different owners, raced each other from the Broomielaw to Rothesay. The sale of the three of them in the following year for blockade running in the US Civil War brought to an end that era of racing.

Racing continued from time to time when two steamers were scheduled to leave a pier at the same time for the next pier and was noted by *Largs* and *Venus* from Arran to Wemyss Bay in 1865 and by *Columba* and *Lord of the Isles* from Rothesay to Colintraive in the late 1880s. Photographs show *Sultan* and *Chancellor* racing off Craigmore, each with large plumes of smoke streaming from her funnel.

The problems caused by steamers racing for piers were such that in 1889 a unique method of pier signalling was introduced following a competition won by Charles Allan of the Allan Line, operators of ocean liners to Canada.

There follows a description of the Signalling Apparatus from James Williamson's *The Clyde Passenger Steamer*:

The Signalling Apparatus, as shown on the diagram, consists of a triangular box raised above the level of the pier to such height as is necessary. One corner of the box faces the water, and the two adjoining sides are set at the most suitable angle for each particular pier, so as to face the line of approach of steamers to each side of the pier. The sides of the box are painted white, and each exposed side contains three circular openings in a horizontal row, the edges of the openings being painted black. Behind each of these openings, a sliding board

Columba and the 1891 *Lord of the Isles* racing in 1910 in Loch Fyne.

Sultan in Williamson colours prior to her sale to the GSWR in 1890 and *Chancellor* of 1880 in Lochgoil colours after 1885, racing, both burning copious amounts of coal, off Greenock.

is arranged to show through the openings, black when let down and white when pulled up. The black parts have small red glass centres, and the white parts have white glass centres.

The intention is that the row of three discs facing approaching steamers should be the signals to three steamers approaching in these relative positions, namely, the inshore signal for the inshore steamer, the middle signal for the middle steamer, and the outside signal for the outside steamer. When the pier is blocked against the approach of any steamer, all the discs show black ; but when it is intended to open the pier to any steamer — by day — the disc corresponding to her position is changed to show white. This is done by pulling the cord attached to the special disc, which locks all the other discs, so that no other signal can be shown while the first is exhibited.

A three steamer race with three GSWR steamers. *Marquis of Bute* is about to be passed by *Neptune* and *Chancellor* is drawing ahead in the background, racing off Greenock in the evening commuter rush to the coast.

The race has finished as the victorious steamer approaches the pier, Craigmore in this instance, with a North British steamer arriving and another from the same fleet not far behind her.

At night a light shows through the red glass centres of the black discs, and through the white glass centre of any disc which may be pulled up, and the discs so lighted are used at night in the same way as the unlighted discs are used during the day.

Racing continued to comparatively recent times, with regular races between *Waverley* and *Jeanie Deans* from Dunoon to Gourock and on occasion when *Caledonia* kept the interest going back to the halcyon days.

The Sunday Breakers

Victorian Scotland was a far more God-fearing country than the Scotland of today, and it was unthinkable to break the fourth Commandment to 'Remember the Sabbath Day and Keep it Holy.' The Clyde Steamers, therefore, did not sail on a Sunday with a handful of exceptions, known as the Sunday Breakers. These steamers gained notoriety at the time, not only for desecrating the Sabbath, but for wild scenes of drunkenness and what would today be called binge drinking.

The first Sunday sailings are believed to have been a mail run from Rothesay to Greenock by a steamer of the Glasgow Castle Steam Packet Company, *Dunoon Castle*, *Inverary Castle*, *Rothesay Castle* or *Toward Castle*, advertised in May 1829 to leave Rothesay at 8:30 and return from Greenock at 11:00. It is not known how long this service lasted and Williamson notes that it was not openly for passengers.

The steamer *Queen of Scots* operated Sunday sailings on her regular route to Arrochar on Communion Sundays prior to being sold to operate on Loch Lomond in 1838. These left Glasgow at 5 a.m. and returned in the late evening, much drink having been consumed by many of the passengers.

The first Sunday excursions from Glasgow to the coast were in 1853 with *Emperor* of 1843, operating initially to Kilmun from 10 July, and then to Garelochhead from 1 August. It was there, on 22 August, that a group of about twenty led by the pier proprietor Sir James Colquhoun of Luss barricaded the pier with boxes, barrels and gangways. The first attempt at berthing was frustrated but a second attempt was successful, helped by a fusillade of coal, bottles, potatoes and turnips, which drove those on the pier back to the gate. A number of youths then got ashore from the steamer and removed the barricade, throwing the items into the water, then going to the upper gate and doing likewise there. All this was witnessed by a crowd of locals on the banks of the loch nearby, keen to see the stramash. The *Emperor* returned to Garelochhead the following Sunday, and although both piers were barricaded, again managed to land her passengers. Her sailings were, unlike later Sunday Breakers, not marked by drunkenness and she continued them for the following few years, possibly up to 1862.

The catamaran steamer *Alliance* advertised two Sunday excursions in 1859, on 30 May to Bowling, and on 4 September to Dumbarton.

In 1858, Henry Sharp, one of the main figures in the Sunday breaking trade, placed *Petrel* of 1845 on a Sunday excursion service from Glasgow to the Kyles of Bute. The Forbes-McLellan law in 1853 had banned the sale of alcoholic drink on Sundays, except to bona fide travellers. This did not apply to the Clyde steamers, and the Sunday excursions ended up patronised, not by people aboard to view the scenery, but by those intent on drinking themselves stupid on the original 'booze cruises'. Sharp owned licensed premises in the Gallowgate in Glasgow

An Edwardian humorous postcard of a paddle steamer with a large crowd of passengers.

and saw his steamers as an extension of these premises. On *Petrel*'s first trip on 11 July 1853, such was the demand for spirits that the vessel ran out of glasses and teacups and egg cups, sugar basins and slop bowls, were pressed into service as receptacles for liquor.

It was not only on Sundays that the Clyde steamers were used for drinking, and it was not unusual for passengers to take advantage of cheap fares and start drinking when they left Glasgow and to be carried off, dead drunk, when the steamer returned, or to land at Dunoon and spend their day in the pubs there abusing alcohol. The terms 'steamboats' and 'steaming' entered the Glaswegian vernacular to mean 'extremely drunk'. This was such a problem that, in 1880, the steamer *Ivanhoe* was built to be run as a teetotal steamer.

Eventually, the bars were placed below the main deck in the bowels of the ship, as can be seen today in *Waverley*'s lower bar, and the phrase 'going to see the engines' was a euphemism for 'going down to the bar'. Even today, *Waverley* has to hire security guards on Saturdays to deal with passengers who have imbibed too much alcohol on the sailing from Glasgow to the Kyles of Bute or while ashore at Dunoon or Rothesay.

Petrel remained in the Sunday trade until the end of the 1859 season, and again from 1865 onwards. Sharp, along with Captain Alexander Watson, had another go at running Sunday steamers in 1864 with the then 20-year-old *Cardiff Castle*. Captain Watson was lost in 1865 when his *Arran Castle* was lost on her delivery voyage to London with all hands. In 1866 Henry Sharp was made bankrupt, but came back to the Sunday trade from 1875 with *Dunoon Castle* of 1867, and from 1881 with *Lough Foyle*, ex-*Lochgoil* of 1853, until she was sold to David MacBrayne in 1885 to become their *Loch Ness*. Sharp worked in conjunction with Duncan Dewar, who operated *Marquis of Lorne*, ex-*Victory*, from 1872, and the veteran *Prince of Wales* of 1849 in 1879, while the double-ended former Dublin steamer *Kingstown* was operated by A. McFarlane in 1885.

Victoria of 1886 reintroduced Sunday excursions for A. Dawson Reid from 1897, replaced in 1898 by *Duchess of York*, ex-*Jeanie Deans*, and in 1903 and 1904 by *Lady of the Isles*, formerly the first *Lord of the Isles*, while *Heather Bell* of 1871 ran trips in 1900 for a single season under charter from her South Coast owners.

On 9 May 1897 *Victoria* opened her Sunday cruise programme with a trip to land at Dunoon and on to a cruise round the Cumbraes but the Dunoon Pier Commissioners had passed a bye-law earlier that year banning steamers from calling at the pier on Sundays. There were no pier hands at Dunoon to take the ropes on her outward call, and the twenty passengers who disembarked there on the return journey found the gates locked. The same thing happened on the following Sunday and for the next few weeks passengers were landed by means of small boats. On Sunday 18 July, another attempt was made to land passengers, and the 100 passengers who landed made an attempt to remove the barrier at the gates, but were met by seven or eight police officers trying to hold back the passengers and threatening to beat them with batons, at which point the barrier was broken and the passengers entered the town. Passengers forced the gates again on the following Sunday but on 1 August she disembarked passengers by her own lifeboats at Kirn instead, and did so for the remainder of the season.

It was not until 1909 that regular Sunday services were started to the coast resorts by the railway companies, initially to Rothesay and Dunoon only. It was not until the 1960s that Arran received a regular Sunday service.

The Blockade Runners

The demand for fast, shallow-draught steamers during the US Civil War in the early 1860s resulted in a large number of Clyde paddle steamers making the trip across the Atlantic to run the blockade of the Confederate ports. Not all made it across safely, the first *Iona* of 1855 being run down off Gourock by a new steamer undergoing trials and others being unable to safely cross the Atlantic. Many were captured by Union warships while attempting to enter the narrow channels leading to the Southern ports.

With the outbreak of war in April 1861, Union forces placed a naval blockade on the Confederate ports along 3,500 miles of coastline from Virginia to the Mexican border of Texas. This was intended to prevent the Confederates from obtaining armaments and from exporting cotton to earn money to pay their army. The Union warships, initially at least, were old and slow, and Southern entrepreneurs soon started buying fast, low-profile, shallow-draught paddle steamers from Britain to run the blockade from Bermuda and the Bahamas to Wilmington, North Carolina and Charleston, South Carolina. The approaches to these ports featured a number of shallow channels impenetrable by Union warships and ideal for the shallow-draught Clyde paddle steamers. Most were painted white or grey as a means of camouflage, and deck saloons were removed from any which had them. Initially, the larger cross-channel steamers were purchased for this, but some twenty-six Clyde steamers were purchased for blockade running, two of which were purchased on the stocks and one (*Ardentinny*) which had previously been sold to Londonderry owners, although only nineteen actually ran the blockade and seven of these were captured or wrecked on their first trip to the Southern ports. Only eight made more than two round trips, and only three are known to have survived the war and returned to commercial service.

The Glasgow merchants were, in the main, sympathetic to the Southern cause, and most steamers were reported as sold to 'The Emperor of China', or for 'The South American trade' or some other such alias. The steamers crossed the Atlantic with their cabins filled with coal, and headed for the Southern ports with essential supplies, returning full of cotton. The mill-owners in Lancashire and Scotland thus maintained their supply of raw cotton, and thus many mill workers were able to keep their jobs. The cost of the steamers could easily be recouped with the earnings from a single cargo.

By late 1864 the Civil War was coming to an end, with Wilmington and Charleston no longer accessible by sea. Mobile had been captured and Galveston, Texas was the only accessible port, served from Havana, Cuba. One former West Highland blockade runner, Hutcheson's *Fairy*, ran to Matamoras in Mexico, just over the border from Brownsville, Texas.

The Rothesay steamer *Neptune* of 1861, which had been sold for running the blockade after only two seasons on the Clyde, captured by the Union Navy and put into service in September 1863 as the patrol steamer USS *Clyde*.

Rothesay Castle of 1861, which had been sold for running the blockade, survived the Civil War, was sold to Canadian owners and rebuilt as *Southern Belle* to run from Toronto to Hamilton on Lake Ontario.

The *Rothesay Castle* of 1865 went to Bordeaux, and is seen to the left here as *Gironde-Garonne No. 1ère* at Royan on the Atlantic coast with the similar *Gironde-Garonne No 2*, which was built by H. McIntyre of Paisley in 1880, to the right and a good crowd on the pier.

The blockade finally ended on 23 June 1865, with a total of just under 300 steamers having attempted to break it with around 1,300 trips, of which around 1,000 were successful. 136 steamers were captured and a further eighty-five destroyed. *Mary Anne* had been ordered by Captain Buchanan's Eagle Steamer Company for the Glasgow to Rothesay service and *Hattie* by the Wemyss Bay Steamboat Co.; both were sold on the stocks to run the blockade.

There follows a list of the Clyde steamers that were sold for blockade running, with the number of runs done and their fate:

Craignish Castle	1844	No record, probably sank on delivery voyage across Atlantic	
Dolphin	1844	Captured before reaching Nassau	Became patrol vessel
Scotia	1845	2.5 round trips	Captured
Star	1849	1 round trip	
Richmond, ex-*Prince Albert*	1850	Wrecked on first inward trip	

Ardentinny/ *Golden Pledge*	1851	Lost before she left UK	
Eagle/Jeanette	1852	3.5 round trips	Sold, did another 2 round trips to Galveston
Diamond	1853	Captured on first inward trip	
Gem	1854	2 round trips	
Iona (I)	1855	Sank off Gourock	
Jupiter	1856	Captured on first inward trip	
Caledonia	1856	1.5 round trips from Bermuda	
Alliance	1857	Captured on first inward trip	
Spunkie	1857	4.5 round trips	
Kelpie	1857	Lost entering Nassau	
Druid	1857	4 return trips	Survived war
Pearl	1859	Captured on first inward trip	
Juno	1860	1 inward trip, used at Charleston, lost on outward trip	
Mail/Susanna	1860	Captured on return voyage, sold and made 5.5 return trips to Galveston	
Ruby	1861	Captured on first inward trip	
Neptune	1861	2.5 round trips	Became US Navy vessel *Clyde*
Rothesay Castle	1861	2.5 round trips	Became *Southern Belle* at Toronto
Fairy	1861	Ran to Matamoras, Mexico	Survived war, sold at Montevideo
Iona (II)	1863	Sank off Lundy	
Mary Anne	1863	Purchased on stocks; made 2.5 round trips	Sold, renamed *Russia*, abandoned soon after
Hattie	1864	Purchased on stocks; lost on delivery voyage	

Accidents and Losses:
Groundings, Boiler Explosions, etc.

Losses with major loss of life

It has been fortunate that there has been only one disaster with major loss of life occurring to a Clyde paddle steamer over the past 200 years, apart from those lost while on war service.

The worst loss of life occurred on 21 October 1825 when Henry Bell's second *Comet* collided with *Ayr* off Kempock Point at Gourock. *Comet* was returning from Inverness and Fort William and was steaming towards Greenock about 2 or 3 a.m. with no lights showing and with a jib sail obstructing the view forwards. *Ayr* was heading from Ayr to Greenock and had lights showing but could not see *Comet* and the latter cut across her path, resulting in a collision. *Comet* sank in three minutes, with the loss of at least sixty lives and thirteen survivors, while *Ayr* headed for the safety of Greenock with no thought for the victims of *Comet*. She was little damaged and sailed on her scheduled run on the following day. The wreck of *Comet* was raised and her engines salvaged, surviving in the Riverside museum in Glasgow.

Two former Clyde steamers suffered major disasters during the nineteenth century. *Rothesay Castle* of 1816 was wrecked at the entrance to the Menai Straits on 18 August 1831 while en route from Liverpool to Beaumaris in a storm, with only twenty-three survivors out of about 150 on board. *Princess Alice*, formerly *Bute* of the Wemyss Bay railway fleet of 1866, which was in service on the Thames, while returning from a excursion to Sheerness on 3 September 1878, collided with the collier *Bywell Castle* a mile seawards of Woolwich, was sliced in two and sank in five minutes with the loss of all but sixty-nine of the 900 or so passengers on board. This was the worst ever loss of life in any coastal steamer accident in the UK.

Boiler Explosions

As already mentioned in the section on racing, *Earl Grey* suffered a boiler explosion on 24 July 1835 while berthed at Greenock preparing for a race. Six were killed and around twenty injured. She was repaired and returned to service.

In 1839 the boiler of the Inveraray steamer *Argyle* exploded when she was at Renfrew with the loss of one life.

On 21 March 1842 the steamer *Telegraph*, only a year old, was destroyed by a catastrophic boiler explosion while departing Helensburgh for Rosneath, having previously arrived from Glasgow and Greenock, with the loss of eighteen lives immediately, a further seven succumbing later to their injuries. The steamer was totally destroyed, with no piece more than a few feet in length surviving

A contemporary drawing of the *Princess Alice* disaster on the Thames on 3 September 1878, probably the worst peace-time disaster to happen to a coastal pleasure steamer in British history.

and the engine and boiler tubes being blown a considerable distance inland, fortunately without hitting anybody, or anything of importance. Surprisingly, there were a number of survivors, with six being taken to Greenock later that day by *Royal Tar*, there to be taken to the infirmary, while a further two, along with two onlookers who had been on the pier, were taken on to Glasgow.

West Highland Losses

The treacherous waters of the West Highlands have been the graveyard of a number of steamers over the years in the era before radar and GPS, from Henry Bell's first *Comet*, which was wrecked on Craignish Point on 15 December 1820, onwards.

On 14 January 1828 *Stirling Castle*, operated by Henry Bell on the Glasgow to Inverness route as a replacement for the second *Comet*, was wrecked in Inverscadail (also known as Inverscaddle) Bay near Ardgour after an engine failure. A clan chief's butler was killed and clan chief McDonnell of Glengarry died later of injuries sustained during the shipwreck.

Hutcheson's *Lapwing* of 1848 was sunk after a collision with Martin Orme's *Islesman* on 22 February 1859 off Glenbervie, Kintyre.

Hutcheson's *Duke of Argyll* of 1852 was accidentally sunk in the Sound of Mull on 12 January 1852, being later raised and beached alongside Salen Pier on 15 March of that year; she was then towed to the Clyde and broken up by the beginning of December.

Hutcheson's first *Chevalier* was wrecked on the Iron Rock in the Sound of Jura on 23 November 1854 when only a year old and became a total wreck.

The little cargo paddler *Carradale* ran ashore at Luing in 1866, but was salvaged and then converted to a screw steamer and moved to the Forth.

Clansman of 1855 was wrecked on Deep Island off Sanda on 21 July 1869 in thick fog.

MacBrayne's *Cygnet* of 1848 was wrecked at Lochailort in 1882, where she had been sent for a cargo of wood. Their first *Mountaineer* of 1852 ran aground on Lady Rock, off the south end of Lismore, on 27 September 1889 at high tide and found herself stranded on the top of the rock when the tide went down.

The second *Islay* of 1867 was wrecked at Red Bay on the Antrim Coast in December 1890, probably while en route to Portrush.

MacBrayne's *Brigadier* was wrecked near Rodel on 7 December 1896 while relieving *Lochiel* on the Outer Islands service from Portree.

The third *Islay*, formerly the Stranraer–Larne steamer *Princess Louise*, was wrecked on Sheep Island, Port Ellen on 15 July 1902 in fog.

MacBrayne's *Glendale*, built in 1875 as *Paris* for the Newhaven to Dieppe service, was wrecked on Cove Point on the Mull of Kintyre on 20 July 1905 while en route from Glasgow to Port Ellen.

The Loch Ness mail steamer *Gairlochy*, ex-*Sultan*, was destroyed by fire at Fort Augustus on Christmas Eve 1919; the remains of her hull were sunk and could be seen for many years under the clear water of Loch Ness, near Fort Augustus pier.

The Staffa and Iona steamer *Grenadier* of 1886 was destroyed by fire while lying overnight at Oban on the night of 5/6 September 1927, with the loss of three of her crew.

MacBrayne's *Chevalier* aground on Barmore Island, near Tarbert, after her starboard paddle wheel fractured during a gale and she ran aground on 25 March 1927.

Mountaineer doing what it says on the tin! Aground on Lady Rock off the south end of Lismore on 27 September 1889 after the tide had gone down.

Clyde Casualties

The former Tay steamer *Oscar* of 1814, on the Lochgoilhead service, was wrecked at Rosneath in 1831.

The Castle Company's *Tarbert Castle*, only a few months old, was wrecked in a storm in Kilfinan Bay in Loch Fyne on 17 January 1839.

Young's *Countess of Eglinton* of 1844 was blown from her mooring at Millport Pier on 27 March of the following year and was wrecked on the Eileans.

McKellar's *Eclipse* of 1850 on the Glasgow to Kilmun service was steered onto the Gantocks on 2 September 1854 by, according to McQueen, 'crass stupidity and inattention' and broke her back before she could be salvaged.

The Stranraer steamer *Briton* of 1847 hit a rock and was lost off Ballantrae on 31 January 1855.

The Millport steamer *Mars* of 1845 was blown ashore at Largs in a storm on 10 April 1855 and wrecked at the mouth of the Gogo Burn.

On Monday 8 October 1855, Captain Bob Campbell's *Duchess of Argyle* was arriving at Glasgow from Garelochhead when, instead of the engines being stopped, they were placed full ahead and the steamer wedged itself under the arches of Glasgow Bridge, removing the funnel and paddle boxes. Captain MacPherson had a fit and later died. On the previous Saturday, on her outward voyage, the engineer was so drunk after leaving Helensburgh that he could not operate the engines, and violently opposed anybody who attempted to enter the engine room and help him. He was eventually overpowered and tied up until the steamer reached Garelochhead. It is possible that he was still under the influence when the steamer reached Glasgow a couple of days later.

Keith & Campbell's Glasgow and Kilmun steamer *Vesta* of 1853 was destroyed by fire on 2 March 1886 while lying at Ardnadam Pier.

Gillies & Campbell's *Lady Gertrude* of 1872 was wrecked while berthing at Toward Pier on 13 January 1877 after her engines failed to reverse, her engines being salvaged and fitted in *Adela*.

MacBrayne's *Chevalier* of 1866 was wrecked on Barmore Island near Tarbert, Loch Fyne on 25 March 1927 after a fracture of the starboard paddle wheel during a gale while on winter relief service on the Ardrishaig mail run. She was salvaged and towed to Troon for demolition.

Clyde groundings

Of a number of occurrences of steamers which ran aground in Clyde water, but later returned to service, we can mention:

Redgauntlet, which ran aground on the Iron Rocks, off the South Coast of Arran, on 14 August 1893 and was refloated ten days later.

Duchess of Fife, which ran aground off Kirn in summer 1938.

Caledonia in 1957 in the Kyles of Bute, following which she was out of service for a large part of the season while she was repaired.

Marchioness of Lorne in 1946 at Kilcreggan.

Talisman in 1948.

Waverley (1947), at Arrochar in 1947 when she was only a week old, at Dunoon near the Rock Café in 1952, at Arrochar in 1971, and on the Gantocks, off Dunoon, in her third year of preservation, on 15 July 1977. She was freed and towed to Dunoon Coal Pier, and was then taken to dry dock for repairs after inspection. She also grounded in the Horseshoe Bend in the River Avon in 1997 and in 2010 off Clevedon Pier.

It must also be made clear that on the approaches to Craigendoran and Helensburgh piers at low water, the NBR, LNER and CSP steamers frequently touched bottom. This was regarded as par for the course and there was never a fuss nor a major issue made out of it, although Helensburgh, up to the closure of the pier in 1952, had a note in the timetable stating 'not at low water'.

It is fortunate that none of these shipwrecks, apart from the second *Comet*, *Stirling Castle*, *Earl Grey*, *Telegraph* and *Grenadier*, were attended by loss of life by passengers or crew.

Of the steamers sold off the Clyde for service overseas, a number never reached their destination. The two *Ionas* have already been mentioned in the section on the Blockade Runners, one being sunk off Gourock and the other off Lundy.

Gleniffer of 1831 was wrecked at Lamorna Cove, Cornwall, en route from Glasgow to Dartmouth on 2 May 1836. It is unclear if she was then trading to the south-west of England or if she was on her delivery voyage to a new owner there.

Argyle of 1838 was wrecked in the Gulf of Mexico on 4 December 1848.

Rothesay Castle of 1837 was wrecked at St Thomas in the Caribbean in February 1857 while travelling out to new owners in Australia under sail.

Redgauntlet ashore on the Iron Rocks in southern Arran on 14 August 1893.

Victoria of 1850 was lost off the island of Anholt in the Kattegat while on her delivery voyage to Russia in September 1859.

Glasgow Citizen of 1852, which had gone out to Australia in 1854, was lost on her delivery voyage to New Zealand on 11 October 1862, where she was heading because of a gold rush.

Osprey of 1852, which had been sold to the Pacific Steam Navigation Co. a couple of years later, was lost after leaving Bermuda, on her way to Peru, where she was due to take up a coastal service.

The railway steamer *Dunoon* of 1852, which had been sold to Australian owners and renamed *Geelong*, sank in the Bay of Biscay on 14 November of that year on her delivery voyage.

Flamingo of 1853, renamed *Bell Bird*, sank in mid-Atlantic on 22 December 1853 on her delivery voyage to Australia.

Eva of 1853 sank off Lambey Island near Dublin on 27 December of that year, on her delivery voyage to Australia.

The pioneer steel-hulled steamer *Windsor Castle* of 1859 ran aground off Sanda on her delivery voyage to India under sail on 27 September 1860.

Ruby of 1860 was lost off the Copeland Islands in November of that year while on her way under sail to a new career in India.

Arran Castle of 1864 sank with all hands after a boiler explosion off Portpatrick on her delivery voyage to the Thames on 22 March 1866.

Lennox of 1864 ran aground near Kingstown (Dun Laoghaire) on her delivery voyage under sail to Brazil on 17 March 1867.

Leven of 1864 sank on her delivery voyage to Bahia, Brazil three days later off the Irish Coast.

Vesper of 1866 sank off St Ives on her delivery voyage to Brazil on 19 January 1867.

Guinevere was lost with all hands in a hurricane in the Bay of Biscay while on her delivery voyage to Constantinople in 1892, witnessed by the crew of a Clan Liner who could do nothing to help.

Unusual and Experimental Steamers

The Clyde paddle steamers have had their fair share of experimental and unusual propulsion systems and hull forms over the past 200 years, especially in the early years of steam navigation.

The first *Comet* had two paddles on each side, geared to a central shaft. After a few weeks the rear pair of paddles was removed, which also helped the steering of the steamer. As far as is known other steamers had the paddles connected directly to the paddle shaft, apart from G. & J. Burns' Belfast steamer *Antelope* of 1833, which operated to the West Highlands from 1838 to 1845 and whose engine was noted as 'geared', as were those of the Glasgow and Stranraer steamer *Caledonia* of 1856 and the Southampton-built *Culzean Castle*, ex-*Windsor Castle* of 1892.

The second steamer built on the Clyde, *Elizabeth*, was sold to Liverpool owners in 1815 to operate from there to Runcorn. In 1818 she was renamed *Safety*; her engines were removed and replaced by a horse-powered treadmill, but this was not a success because the horses got seasick.

The four steamers on the Forth & Clyde Canal in the 1830s were all stern-wheel propelled; *Cyclops*, originally a horse-drawn 'Swift' boat built in 1825, which was fitted with an engine in 1829, and *Lord Dundas* of 1831 both had a stern wheel in a central trough, similar to that of the pioneer steam vessel *Charlotte Dundas*, which had been built in 1801 as a tug, but which had been prohibited from operating on the canal because of fears of damage to the canal banks by her wash. *Manchester* of 1832 had a central engine and two wheels on the stern quarters, as had *Edinburgh* of 1832, a design that was later used on steamers built for African rivers and for a class of steamers built for the Mesopotamian campaign in the First World War. These designs were clearly to avoid the problems associated with conventional side wheels making a steamer too wide for the canal. The Swedes got round this by placing the paddle wheels inboard in what were known as 'fiddle-steamers' for use on the Göta Canal, as can be seen in the recently built replica *Eric Nordevall II*. *Edinburgh* was converted to side wheel propulsion in December 1833 when she was converted for use as a tug at Grangemouth.

The only conventional stern wheel steamer on the Clyde was David Napier's *Kilmun* of 1851, built at Worcester and with his experimental rotary engine fitted. She had run on the Severn at Worcester, named *Severn*, and was brought up to the Clyde for the Glasgow to Kilmun service in 1863, but only operated for a week. Sadly, as far as is known, no illustrations have survived of this unique vessel.

In 1853 David Napier built a conventional paddle steamer with his rotary engine, named *Rotary*. No drawings appear to have survived for this engine, but it appears to have had two horizontal cylinders connected to the paddle shaft. Williamson states:

Lord of the Isles of 1877 when in service on the Thames, at St Paul's Wharf on the Thames above London Bridge, between 1891 and 1898. She had been fitted with telescopic funnels to pass under London Bridge, and the fore funnel is partially collapsed in this view.

Rolls-Royce *Lucy*, as used for experimental jet propulsion trials in 1950 and 1951.

She was furnished with a surface-condenser in the form of a tank placed under the machinery. This tank was filled with tubes, to which sea-water was admitted and discharged through apertures in the shell plating. The boiler was of the 'water- tube' type. It had double rows of tubes placed diagonally, and wrought, under the forced draught principle, at the pressure, remarkable in those days, of 120 lbs. per square inch. The furnace bars were also circulating tubes, and each was fitted with a cock to draw off any deposit. These water-tube fire bars, together with the forced draught, were patented by Napier in 1851. The rotary engine, from which the boat took its name, proved hardly so great a success. It appears to have consisted of one long cylinder in two compartments, 'through which the paddle shaft passed.'

Andrew McQueen states in *Echoes of Old Clyde Paddle Wheels* that steering was by a horizontal wheel and that there were two long, iron handles coming up from the engine room to the bridge, thus giving bridge control of the engines, something that has not been really developed on a paddle steamer until recent years on Lake Geneva in Switzerland. *Rotary* was placed on the route from Glasgow to Dumbarton, but was not a success. The rotary engine was replaced after only a few weeks in service and the steamer was fitted with diagonal oscillating engines and renamed *Dumbarton*, returning to service in 1855 and later serving as *Gareloch* from 1860 onwards.

In 1857 another experimental steamer, *Alliance*, was built. Designed by George Mills and built by Tod & McGregor, she was intended to have improved stability through the use of twin hulls, improved manoeuvrability by use of a single central paddle wheel between the hulls, and improved accommodation with the use of deck saloons. The twin hulls had normal curves on the outside and straight lines on the inside. The main deck covered the width of both hulls with the paddle wheel covered by the paddle box protruding through it. At each end of the central trough were small paddle wheels, powered by donkey engines, which could be rotated and were intended to be used for steering. She was also double-ended, a feature which did not reach the Clyde generally until the modern car ferries, long after the era of the paddle steamer. A model of her in Merseyside Maritime Museum shows four funnels, two on each hull, but contemporary accounts state that she had only two funnels After a few years' experimental work by her designer, she was ordered in 1856. She had two trunk engines, one in each hull. Running trials in December 1856, she entered service the following April to Garelochhead. She gained a reputation as being a slow steamer and was not successful in spite of the comfort of her deck saloons, and from August 1857 she was transferred to the Lochgoilhead service. The lack of custom led to her owners going into liquidation at the end of 1858. In 1859 the liquidator chartered her out for a handful of Sunday-breaking sailings; she did not sail in 1860, and in 1861 she operated for a short season on the Caledonian Canal from the end of June on charter to David Hutcheson. In 1863 she was sold to Liverpool owners and was sent blockade-running after alterations during which she was converted to a conventional paddle steamer: the deck salons were removed and replaced by whalebacks fore and aft, the engines upgraded or replaced (according to different sources), a stern was added and she received three funnels side-by-side. Captured in April 1864 on her first trip, she was sold at auction to Boston owners and sent to Melbourne, Australia. After a brief stay at Melbourne, she sailed for New Zealand, where gold had recently been found in the South Island, and she was renamed *New Zealand*. She made one successful return journey from

Dunedin to Lyttleton, but was wrecked at the entrance to Hokitika Harbour, the port nearest the goldfields, on the second trip on 7 August 1865. Some reports state that her engines were salvaged and taken to Melbourne.

Kingstown was another double-ended steamer with deck saloons. She had previously run from Dublin to Kingstown, now Dun Laoghaire. She had a very short career on the Clyde, serving as a Sunday-breaker in 1885 and 1886.

Other unusual steamers included:

Albion of 1816, in which the height of the paddle wheels could be adjusted depending on the amount of cargo carried, and which had two funnels side by side;

Highland Lad, ex-*Defiance* of 1817, which had experimental chain paddle floats fitted in 1826 at the end of her career;

Queen of Beauty of 1844, which was originally fitted with 'Kibble's Patent Chain Floats' with a chain and one paddle shaft powered by the engines, and the other end of the chain round a drum, somewhat like a modern bulldozer drive. This proved to be too noisy, to create too much friction and damaged the paddle box; it was replaced after a few weeks by conventional paddles which afforded an extra two knots of speed. This was invented by John

An unusual visitor berthed at Craigendoran during the Second World War, *Fair Maid* from the Forth; previously Buchanan's *Isle of Skye* and built for in 1886 Bob Campbell of Kilmun as *Madge Wildfire*, she had served in the CSP fleet under that name from 1888 until 1911. She was used as a decontamination vessel during the war years but had a week replacing *Lucy Ashton* in spring 1944, and is seen here dressed for VE Day in 1945.

Another paddle visitor at Craigendoran. This is the diesel-hydraulic paddle car ferry *Sir William Wallace*, which had been built by Dennys at Dumbarton for the Queensferry Passage on the Forth in 1955. She was at Craigendoran during her trials and while awaiting her delivery voyage to the Forth and is sharing the pier with the motor vessel *Maid of Cumbrae*.

Kibble, later to build the Kibble Palace at Coulport, now in Glasgow's Botanic gardens and the photographer of the famous early view of the Broomielaw with so many paddle steamers in it.

The paddle yacht *Comet* was also unusual, in terms of steam yachts as well as Clyde steamers. She operated short trips out of Rothesay in 1893 but was destroyed by fire at her owner's shipyard at Alloa in the following March. At only 87 feet long, she was very much a miniature Clyde steamer.

The diesel-electric paddler *Talisman* of 1935 was also an experimental steamer. Externally a normal-looking Clyde steamer, the replacement of steam reciprocating by diesel-electric machinery was revolutionary and had the machinery been more reliable, and had the Second World War not broken out, more such vessels would have been built for Clyde service to replace the aging veteran paddle steamers, some dating from the nineteenth century.

Imports

Also unusual were the small number of paddle steamers brought to the Clyde or West Highlands after previous service elsewhere. Practically all Clyde steamers were built and engined on the Clyde for service there, initially at least. Those that came from other waters were:

• *Oscar*, built in 1814 at Dundee as *Tay* for the route from Dundee to Perth, which was on the Lochgoilhead service from 1818.

• *Stirling Castle*, built in 1814 for service on the Forth from Stirling to Newhaven and Dysart, and purchased in 1820 by Robert Napier for service on Loch Ness, and on the Caledonian Canal when that was opened throughout in 1822.

• *Duke of Lancaster*, built in 1822 for service from Liverpool and purchased in 1826 as the first steamer of the Campbeltown & Glasgow Steam Packet Joint Stock Company for the Glasgow to Campbeltown service.

• *West Highland Steamers* records that a steamer named *Colonsay*, which was on West Highland service in 1834, was the renamed *Glasgow*, built by R. Duncan in 1834 and previously operating from Dublin to Kingstown.

• G. & J. Burns' Glasgow to Liverpool steamer *Gazelle* of 1822 was sold to John Fleming in 1838 and ran from Glasgow to Inverness for a short period, while their *Antelope* of 1833 was transferred to the North British Steam Navigation Co. and ran from Glasgow to the West Highlands from 1838 to 1845.

• The City of Glasgow Steam Packet Co.'s *Vulcan* of 1833 on the Glasgow to Belfast service was transferred to the West Highland services of Thomson & McConnell in 1838, serving there until 1840.

• *Foyle* of 1829 from the Glasgow to Londonderry service ran cruises from Glasgow and Londonderry to the West Highlands at the Glasgow Fair each year, and was chartered to Thomson & McConnell to run from Glasgow to Portree and Islay in April and May 1842.

• *Falcon* of 1835, under Irish ownership and on the Belfast to Liverpool service, was purchased by Sir James Matheson of Stornoway in 1845 and offered a service from Ardrossan to Stornoway via Campbeltown, Port Ellen, Oban, Tobermory and Portree but she only operated on the route from October of that year until June of the following year, replaced by *Mary Jane*, later to become the long-lived *Glencoe*.

• *Modern Athens* of 1836, which had been built for the Leith to Dundee service, was purchased by John Ramsay of Islay in 1846 for the Glasgow and West Loch Tarbert to Port Ellen services, which she maintained until 1849.

• *Glow Worm* of 1838, built as a yacht for Thomas Assheton Smith in 1838 and sold for use on the Ardrossan to Belfast service, was used for a Glasgow to Stornoway service in the summers of 1851, 1853 and 1855.

• David Napier's stern wheel steamer *Kilmun*, which ran from Glasgow to Kilmun for only a week in 1863, had previously operated on the Bristol Channel in 1859 and the River Severn from 1860 to 1862.

• *Vale of Clwyd* of 1865 spent her first year in service running from Liverpool to Rhyl; she kept her Welsh name when on the Clyde from 1866 to 1880, and after she was sold to Thames owners until she was scrapped in 1888, although she was advertised when on the Clyde as *Vale of Clyde* and known as such by the general public.

• The North British Steam Packet's steamer *Carham* was built in 1864, and ran on the Solway from Silloth to Dumfries and Annan for the first three years of her life. She only spent three years on the Clyde and was then sold to the Highland Railway and on to owners in Bournemouth in 1880.

• *Ondine*, on the Ullapool to Stornoway service from 1871 to 1877 for Sir James Matheson, had been built as a Royal Mail steamer for the Dover to Calais service in 1844 and was purchased in the late 1850s by the *Morning Herald* newspaper to get despatches from the Continent quickly from Calais to Dover so that the news was as up to date as possible.

• *Lisboa*, built in 1860 for the service from Lisbon to Oporto, was purchased in 1873 by the Western Isles Steam Packet Co. Ltd., part-owned by John McCallum, later to operate *Hebrides*, and whose company became part of McCallum Orme, and renamed *Saint Clair of the Isles*. She was operated from Glasgow to the Outer Isles and was sold at auction in 1875, later serving in the Dutch East Indies as *Mangkoe Almansoer*.

• The double-ended steamer *Kingstown* of 1863, as mentioned above, was purchased in 1885 for use as a Sunday breaker, but lasted little more than a year on the Clyde.

• *Cygnus* of 1854, which initially ran from Harwich to Antwerp, then from 1857 to 1889 from Weymouth to the Channel Islands, and in 1890 on excursions from Southport, was purchased in 1891 by David MacBrayne, running in that year on the Inveraray cargo service. Renamed *Brigadier* in 1892 and then placed on the Oban to Loch Sunart service, she was later used on various relief sailings and was wrecked near Rodel on 7 December 1896.

• *Great Western* was built in 1867 for a service from Milford to Cork, and was taken over by the Great Western Railway five years later, continuing to serve on this route and from Weymouth to Cherbourg and to the Channel Islands until 1891 when, after a brief period of ownership at Preston, she was purchased by David MacBrayne, by whom she was renamed *Lovedale* from 1893 and served Stornoway and, for a short spell, Islay, until broken up in 1904.

• Another MacBrayne purchase, in 1893, was *Albert Edward* of 1878, from the Portsmouth to Ryde joint railway service. She became *Carabinier* for MacBrayne and served on the Oban to Loch Sunart service until scrapped in 1908.

• *Windsor Castle* was a large paddle steamer built in 1892 to compete with Cosens on excursions out of Bournemouth. Three years later she was sold to the Clyde and, renamed *Culzean Castle*, spent three years on a Princes Pier–Fairlie–Campbeltown service and was then sold to Clyde Excursion Steamers Ltd for excursion work as *Carrick Castle* in 1899. In 1900 she was sold to a Russian-owned railway company in China, and was captured by the Japanese in the Russo-Japanese war in 1904 and served on Japan's Inland Sea until she ran aground in 1931.

• In 1898 the Glasgow & South Western Railway purchased a steamer which was being built for a Thames operator, most probably Planet Steamers, which had been operating the first *Lord of the Isles* under the name *Jupiter*. She went on the Ayr Excursion service as *Juno*, serving there until 1932.

• MacBrayne's *Glendale*, purchased in 1902 for the Glasgow to Islay service to replace the wrecked *Islay*, ex-*Princess Louise*, had started life as *Paris* on the Newhaven to Dieppe service for the London, Brighton & South Coast Railway in 1875. in 1888 she had been taken back by her builders, Fairfield's, in part exchange, was used briefly on excursions from Llandudno in 1890, then chartered to the Hamburg America Line from 1892 to 1895 to operate from Hamburg to Helgoland as *Flamingo*, and in 1897 was on excursions from Tilbury to Ostend as *La Belgique*. Under MacBrayne's ownership she served on the Stornoway Mail service, Oban–Gairloch and Glasgow–Islay services and was wrecked on Deas Point, Kintyre on 20 July 1905.

• *Kylemore* was laid down in 1897 by Captain John Williamson in a fit of enthusiasm, alongside sister *Strathmore*, but he got cold feet and she was sold on the stocks to a Sussex company, operating out of Hastings as *Britannia* until sold back to Williamson in 1904. He then sold her to the Glasgow & South Western Railway, for whom she operated as *Vulcan* until Williamson bought her back in 1908 and sailed her under her original name, mainly on the service from Rothesay in the morning up to Glasgow. She continued under the ownership of Williamson-Buchanan Steamers and the LMSR-owned Williamson-Buchanan Steamers (1936) Ltd until sunk while serving as a minesweeper in 1940.

• In 1905 London County Council built a larger fleet of paddle steamers for a commuter service. This was not a success and ceased running after 1907, although some were sold to private operators and continued on Thames service. In 1914 two of these, *Earl Godwin* and *Shakespeare*, were purchased by the Dumbarton & Balloch Joint Line Committee for use on Loch Lomond, becoming *Queen Mary* and *Princess Patricia* respectively. The former was damaged by fire shortly after arriving on the loch and never entered service, but the latter offered short trips from Balloch until scrapped in 1938.

• P. & A. Campbell's Bristol Channel paddle steamer *Britannia* of 1896 made a visit to the Clyde in 1901 for yacht races in connection with the Glasgow International Exhibition of that year. She sailed from Bristol, Cardiff, Penarth and Mumbles to Gourock on Thursday 6 June, arriving the following morning, made two trips from Gourock and Rothesay to follow the yachts on 7 and 8 June, and sailed back south on Tuesday 11 June in connection with the 08:30 train from Glasgow to Gourock with a cruise to the Gareloch, the Holy Loch, Loch Long, through the Kyles of Bute and along the Arran Coast, proceeding thence back to her home waters, arriving the following day at Mumbles at 09:30, Cardiff at 12:00, and Bristol at 14:00.

A number of Clyde paddle steamers spent brief periods of their careers on services from Ulster ports, mainly on the Belfast to Bangor service or operating from Londonderry to Moville, such as the 1886 *Victoria*, which was from Belfast to Bangor in 1890, the first *Jeanie Deans*, which served on the latter route from 1896 until 1899, and *Lochgoil* of 1853 which served as a tender at Londonderry, named *Lough Foyle* from 1875 until sold back to Clyde owners two years later, for whom she kept her Irish name until sold to David MacBrayne in 1886, for whom she served on the Loch Ness mail service as *Loch Ness* until scrapped in 1912.

The Glory Days of
the Clyde Paddle Steamer: 1889–1914

This section could very easily be seen to rewrite history or go over all the great works written before on a colourful part of Clyde steamer history. With that in mind, this part will gloss over the period from the early 1890s to 1922. If you need to know more we would encourage you to obtain some of the notable works on the subject listed in the Bibliography at the back of this publication.

These golden years were a real delight for the Victorian and Edwardian enthusiast on the Clyde. The variety of steamers and sailings on offer would leave you with the question 'Where do I start?' The sound of the paddles, the white foaming wash, the copious amounts of black smoke and hourly racing seem heaven in today's emptiness on the Firth.

It was without a doubt a period of vision, with the expansion of the various fleets completed within the early 1900s. The Caledonian Steam Packet, based at Gourock, with their routes, the steamers of the Glasgow & South Western Railway and the North British Railway, along with the independent fleets of Williamson and Buchanan and the West Highland steamers of David MacBrayne provided a stream of colour on the Clyde, rivalry was high and trade competitive.

The piers of the Firth were the heart and soul of the community. Everything came in and went out by steamer. People went to work by steamer (one of the authors remembers a schoolteacher in the early 1960s who commuted from Dunoon to Paisley), went to family occasions by steamer and many holidayed on the steamers with a variety of runabout tickets on offer. These still continued until the 1970s, and today with the new 2012 'Friends of *Waverley*'.

To cope with the many vessels calling at piers, a bull's-eye semaphore system was installed at most piers, which allowed the piermaster control of those arriving at his berths (see the section on Racing for more details). You can still see these at Kilcreggan and Dunoon today, although they are no longer in use. Pointing porters helped folks to their accommodation from the steamers, and from the 1930s loudspeaker systems were used to announce the many ships and cruises on offer at the larger piers. LP records were played all day at Dunoon, Rothesay and Campbeltown, including Jimmy Shand and the Jim MacLeod Scottish Dance Band, adding greatly to the atmosphere on the pier. Tearooms and upper decks made visits to them attractive; indeed, to watch the steamers became a hobby.

As well as the many paddle steamers, the view, in particular on good days, from Dunoon Pier allowed you to watch all kinds of shipping on the Firth, from transatlantic liners to the humble puffer, from warships on patrol to ships built on the river running their trials. From 1901 the turbine steamers added a new form of Clyde steamer to excite the onlooker.

A commemorative cover and postmark celebrating 80 years of the Caledonian Steam Packet Co. in 1969, issued by the Clyde River Steamer Club, designed by Robin B. Boyd.

Dunoon Pier with the GSWR's *Mercury* at Berth2 and the CSP's *Duchess of Montrose* at Berth 1. The pier is little altered today.

Arrochar, unusually with four steamers berthed, from an album of photographs taken by the contractors building the West Highland Line. From the left can be seen *Chancellor* in GSWR colours, the NB's *Lady Rowena*, the GSWR's *Neptune* and the CSP's *Marchioness of Lorne*.

Arrochar between 1922 and 1927 with the 1899 *Waverley* and MacBrayne's *Iona*, then on the Lochgoilhead mail service.

Waverley berthed on the outside of Millport Pier in CalMac colours in 1973.

Rothesay Pier in an image from a lantern slide, probably from the 1870s, with what is probably *Athole* (1866) lying across the end of the pier.

Rothesay in a pre-1910 postcard view with *Kenilworth* departing, *Marchioness of Breadalbane* across the west end of the pier and *Columba* arriving.

Rothesay pier in pre-1923 days with *Jupiter* departing and the 1899 *Waverley* berthed along the pier.

The western end of Rothesay Pier with *Ivanhoe* berthed across the end, *Columba* arriving and *Eagle III* and *Duchess of Rothesay* along the front of the pier.

By the outbreak of war in 1914 the zenith was over; indeed, from 1908 the CSP and the GSWR had operated pooled sailings, especially on the Ardrossan to Arran service, a measure introduced to avoid profit-consuming competition, with each company's steamers being used in alternate years on the Arran service. The 1920s and 1930s still allowed the river to be a hobby, a holiday and generally a place you wanted to go to and the resorts offered the holidaymaker plenty to do, with children's shows, summer season shows and lots of cruising ideas. Many inhabitants of industrial Clydeside either owned or rented flats in the Firth resorts where they spent the summer months. The weather, well, that played its ugly hand and did much to kill the Clyde off, although this period did its best to continue those traditions of the golden era.

Serving their Country:
The First World War

From the start of the First World War in 1914 it was soon realised that the coastal and excursion paddle steamer, with its shallow draught, made an ideal minesweeper. A total of twenty-five Clyde paddle steamers and one West Highland paddle steamer served their country during that conflict, with four being lost through enemy action and a further two not returning to Clyde service after the war. Those utilised were:

Caledonian Steam Packet

• *Caledonia*: April 1917 to April 1919; minesweeper based at Spithead, also carried troops from Le Havre to Paris at the end of the war; returned to Clyde service 20 November 1919.
• *Marchioness of Breadalbane*: April 1917 to May 1919; renamed HMS *Marquis of Breadalbane*; minesweeper, first at Troon, later at Portsmouth, returned to Clyde service, 2 June 1919.
• *Duchess of Hamilton*: February to November 1915; troop transport sailing across the Channel from Southampton, minesweeper from September 1915, lost on 29 November 1915 after striking a mine off Harwich.
• *Marchioness of Lorne*: January 1917 to March 1921; minesweeper based at Port Said, delayed on her return from there, spending a lot of time at Gibraltar. She was laid up after her return and sold in 1923 for scrapping.
• *Duchess of Rothesay*: October 1915 to April 1919; minesweeper renamed HMS *Duke of Rothesay*, based at Sheerness and later at Portland, towed a disabled Zeppelin into Margate; swept more than 500 mines; returned to Clyde service 1920.
• *Duchess of Montrose*: February 1915 to March 1917; troop transport sailing across the Channel from Southampton, minesweeper from May 1915, renamed HMS *Montrose*, mined off the French coast on 18 March 1917 and lost.
• *Duchess of Fife*: April 1917 to April 1919; minesweeper, renamed HMS *Duchess*, based mainly at Grimsby; returned to service 8 September 1919.

The CSP, having had their entire fleet depart for war service, relied on chartered tonnage to maintain their services from 1917 to the end of the war, including *Ivanhoe* and *Benmore* from the Williamson fleet, and *Iona*, *Chevalier* and *Fusilier* from David MacBrayne.

Glasgow & South Western Railway

• *Neptune*: 1915 to April 1917; minesweeper, based at Dover, renamed HMS *Nepaulin*; blown up and sunk near the Dyck Light Vessel, 20 April 1917.
• *Glen Sannox*: 1916; troop transport Southington to France; made only one trip then returned to her owners as unsuitable.
• *Mercury*: 1915 to April 1919; minesweeper, during which she was damaged twice, first having her stern blown off and then losing her bow only a day after she returned to service after the first incident; returned to Clyde service 1920.
• *Minerva*: 1915 to 1920; Admiralty patrol paddler, then a minesweeper, renamed *Minerva II*, based at Malta, said to have been at the Gallipoli landings and to have sailed from Salonika to Mudros in 1916. Claimed to have been sold to Turkish owners and remained in Lloyds Register until 1927 with no owner's name listed, but Turkish records do not mention her and it was possible she was scrapped or lost.
• *Glen Rosa*, May 1917 to April 1919; minesweeper, renamed HMS *Glencross*; based on Belfast Lough; returned to service 17 September 1919.
• *Jupiter*: 1915 to April 1919; minesweeper, renamed *Jupiter II*, worked off Dover; returned to service 1920.
• *Juno*: January 1915 to 1919; minesweeper, renamed HMS *Junior*, initially on the Firth of Clyde between Ardrossan and Brodick, then on the Firth of Forth, based at Granton; returned to service 28 June 1919.
• *Mars*: September 1916 to November 1918; minesweeper, renamed HMS *Marsa*, run down by a destroyer on 18 November 1918 at the approaches to Harwich Harbour, her back was broken, she settled on a sandbank, broke in two during salvage attempts and became a total loss.

The GSWR was also left without tonnage in 1917 and 1918 and Buchanan's *Isle of Cumbrae*, MacBrayne's *Gael* and *Glencoe* and Turbine Steamers' *Lord of the Isles* were chartered at different periods.

North British Railway

• *Talisman*: September 1917 to February 1919; minesweeper, renamed HMS *Talla*, first from Troon, later from Portsmouth, returned to the Clyde on 26 February 1919; returned to service 10 October 1919.
• *Kenilworth*: June 1917 to February 1919; minesweeper, first from Troon, later from Portsmouth, returned to service 3 May 1919.
• *Waverley*: September 1915 to April 1919; minesweeper, based at Sheerness, later at Grimsby, Weymouth, Harwich, Lowestoft, Grimsby, Bournemouth and West Hinden on the Belgian coast.
• *Marmion*: February 1915 to April 1919; minesweeper, renamed HMS *Marmion II*, based at Dover; returned to Clyde service 1920.
• *Fair Maid*: A new steamer which never came into service for the NBR; launched on 23 December 1915; entered service as a minesweeper March 1916; sunk 9 November 1916 near Cross Sands Buoy.

Marmion as a minesweeper 1915–19 showing the sweeping equipment on the stern and the built up bow.

The unfortunate *Fair Maid* of 1915, built as a Clyde paddle steamer but which never saw service as such, being called up for war service while fitting out and sunk after less than a year's service as a minesweeper.

Former North British Steamers

• *Lady Rowena*: owned by A. B. Cameron in 1914; fleet tender at Rosyth and naval hospital carrier on the Forth; sold to owners at Goole, April 1919, did not return to Clyde service, scrapped 1922.
• *Lady Clare*: owned by Moville Steamship Co. in 1914; minesweeper based at Belfast.
• *Redgauntlet*: owned by NBR subsidiary Galloway Saloon Steam Packet Co. in 1914; minesweeper based at Grimsby, sold to the Admiralty in 1917; sold by them in April 1919 to Cie de Navires Olivier, Paris and used at Oran.

With *Lucy Ashton* and *Dandie Dinmont* remaining on the Clyde during the conflict, the NB managed without the need to charter in tonnage.

Buchannan Steamers Ltd

• *Isle of Arran*: 1917 to April 1919; minesweeper, based on the Clyde, later at Portsmouth, used as a troop transport from Le Havre and Rouen to Paris in 1918–19. Returned to Clyde service 1920.
• *Eagle III*: 1916 to April 1919; minesweeper based at Grimsby, later at Harwich, from which she made several trips to off the Dutch coast to escort food convoys, returned to Clyde service 1920.
• *Isle of Skye*, ex-*Madge Wildfire*: 1916 to March 1919; tender at Invergordon, also minesweeper in the Pentland Firth. Returned to service 10 May 1919.

Lady Rowena in service as a minesweeper between 1916 and 1919.

John Williamson & Co.

• *Kylemore*: 1915 to 1919; minesweeper in the English Channel, based at Dunkirk and later at Harwich; returned to Clyde service 1920.
• *Queen Empress*: 1915 to November 1919: troop transport from Southampton to French ports, was in collision with a destroyer between Folkestone & Boulogne and was towed to Boulogne by the CSP turbine *Duchess of Argyll*; later a minesweeper based on the Tyne, in 1919 used as an ambulance transport in the White Sea at Archangel in support of the White Russian army, where she ran aground and was just refloated in the nick of time before she was captured by the advancing Bolshevik army; returned to the Clyde on 4 November 1919.

As there was little demand for excursion sailings during the 1914–18 conflict, the all-the-way services of Williamson and Buchanan from the Broomielaw were suspended after 1916, in which year *Isle of Cumbrae* sailed to Dunoon and *Isle of Arran* to the Gareloch, and in 1919 the two companies merged.

David MacBrayne Ltd

• *Grenadier*: July 1916 to October 1919: minesweeper in the North Sea, renamed HMS *Grenade*.

Grenadier as the minesweeper HMS *Grenade* between 1916 and 1919.

Evening Cruises

Evening cruises were offered from the major piers on the Firth with bands on board and were extremely popular. Destinations included the Arran Coast, Millport, the Kyles of Bute and Loch Fyne. A destination invented for the evening cruises was One Tree Island in Loch Riddon, a small islet with a single tree on it. These all ended with the Second World War in 1939. Although the paddle steamers took part with the turbine steamers, the evening cruises became all-weather comfort trips. *Waverley* was involved in evening cruises in 1972 and 1973, as paddle steamers had been in the 1920s and before. *Waverley* still offers occasional 'showboat' evening cruises, mainly downriver from Glasgow rather than from coast resorts, however.

Right: A handbill for an evening cruise from Craigendoran to Dunoon for a special fireworks display on 15 September 1928.

Far right: A handbill for a wide variety of evening cruises by *Kylemore*, described as a 'magnificent steamer' for the last week in July 1928 from Rothesay, during the last week in July 1928 departing from Rothesay and Craigmore.

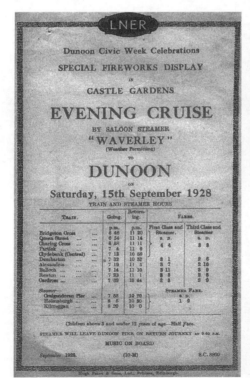

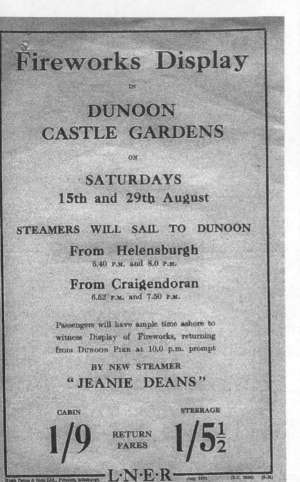

Above left: A handbill for evening cruises to Dunoon for fireworks displays in August 1931, advertising the 'New Steamer *Jeanie Deans*'.

Above right: A handbill for special evening cruises by *Jeanie Deans* from Rothesay on 10 and 14 August 1934.

The 1930s

During the 1890s and the early part of the twentieth century, paddle steamers were of a more or less standard design, modified in some instances with the extension of the promenade deck to the bow (in the CSP's *Duchess of Hamilton*, *Duchess of Rothesay*, *Marchioness of Lorne*, *Duchess of Montrose* and *Duchess of Fife*, Buchanan's *Eagle III* and the Inveraray Company's 1891 *Lord of the Isles* after alterations in 1898), and in a few with a solid section forwards, with the plating extended up to the promenade deck level (the GSWR's *Jupiter*, *Juno*, and *Mars*, Captain John Williamson's *Kylemore*, *Strathmore* and *Queen-Empress*, and the NB's *Waverley* and *Marmion* (briefly) after alterations during war service). Two steamers, *Glenmore* and *Culzean Castle*, had a hybrid design, being plated up at the bow but open at the sides a bit further aft to aid rope handling. Otherwise a deck saloon and open bow predominated as late as *Marmion* in 1906. The 1930s saw all steamers built in that decade plated up at the bow, and all the CSP newbuilds featured streamlining, the buzzword of the decade, and a paddle box with no embellishments and disguised to look like a turbine steamer or motorship. The names, however, continued a long tradition with *Caledonia*, *Mercury*, *Marchioness of Lorne*, *Juno* and *Jupiter*. The LNER continued with traditional paddle boxes on *Jeanie Deans*, *Talisman* and the 1947 *Waverley*, which was designed in 1938. The modern styles did not go down well with the enthusiast fraternity and were heavily criticised during their early days. Ferry paddlers and point to point services allowed them to carry a few cars at a suitable tidal level, thus making them the Firth's first car ferries.

Throughout this period the Clydesiders took to heart the river scene and many, many letters were written on these 1930s paddlers, all unfavourably. Again, an improved class of turbine steamers were built in this decade but these vessels did not cast aside the paddle steamer with only nine entering scheduled service on the Firth and Loch Lomond in the 100 years after *Queen-Empress* in 1912, compared to over 400 in the previous century.

The design of the 1934 twins *Mercury* and *Caledonia* enabled cars to be carried at certain states of the tide, as seen in this 1930s view of a car being loaded onto *Mercury* at Millport.

Caledonia off Rothesay in her inaugural season of 1934.

A stern view of *Caledonia* in Rothesay Bay in the same year with a steam yacht and the LNER's *Marmion* in the background.

The short-lived *Juno* in her first season, 1937.

Serving their Country:
The Second World War

The second major conflict of the twentieth century saw Clyde and West Highland paddle steamers play their part again, and serve with distinction in the evacuation of troops from Dunkirk at the end of May 1940 and at the D-Day landings in June 1944.

Most of the steamers were taken up for war service shortly after the outbreak of war in September 1939, with some being used in the evacuation of children from the city of Glasgow to the safer towns and villages around the Firth of Clyde.

A total of thirteen Clyde paddle steamers and the two remaining West Highland paddle steamers were called up for war service; five were losses due to enemy action, one was stripped of her machinery and saloons and sunk as a blockship and four did not return to service and were scrapped following the conflict.

Paddle steamers used in the Second World War were:

Caledonian Steam Packet

• *Duchess of Rothesay*: 21 September 1939 to 1946; minesweeper on the Clyde and then at Dover, laid up at Portsmouth, then minesweeping at Harwich again; accommodation ship at Brightlingsea from May 1942, beached there October 1945, sold to Holland for breaking up August 1946.
• *Duchess of Fife*: 21 September 1941 to 1946, resumed service 28 May 1946; minesweeper based at Grimsby, later at Dover, where she made four return trips from Ramsgate to the beaches of Dunkirk and rescued a total of over 2,000 troops, including 550 French soldiers; from 1941 she was a training ship for officers and men and used as an experimental minesweeper based at Port Edgar on the Forth until the end of the war. She resumed Clyde service in 1946.
• *Mercury*: October 1939 to 24 December 1940: minesweeper, first on the Clyde and then at Milford Haven; damaged by a mine 24 December 1940, 50 miles out of Milford Haven, and sank while under tow by a trawler.
• *Caledonia*: 21 September 1939 to 1945, resumed service 9 May 1946; minesweeper, on the Clyde and later at Portland and Milford Haven, renamed HMS *Goatfell*; Anti-aircraft ship in the Thames Estuary May 1941 during the Blitz, damaged in the same air raid in which *Juno* was sunk; escort vessel off the east coast between the Tyne and the Humber from July 1941, then at Harwich from 1943 as an escort for buoy tenders; used as a troop transport and patrol vessel, carrying American troops to the D-Day landings on 7 June 1944, then was off

the French coast for a month as an anti-aircraft ship, returned to Portland July 1944 and used as an anti-aircraft ship at Portsmouth against the flying bombs; was in the second group of vessels to reach Antwerp in November 1944.

• *Marchioness of Lorne* remained on the Clyde during the war years, providing an essential service to the inhabitants of Dunoon and the Holy Loch villages.

• *Jupiter*: 21 September 1939 to 1945, resumed service 9 February 1946; minesweeper based on the Clyde, renamed HMS *Scawfell*, then at Portland and at Milford Haven; used as an anti-aircraft vessel in the Thames Estuary from May 1941 during the Blitz; escort vessel off the east coast between the Tyne and the Humber from July 1941, then at Harwich from 1943 as an escort for buoy tenders; used as an anti-aircraft ship off the D-Day beaches June 1944 for a month, returned to Portland July 1944 and used as an anti-aircraft ship at Portsmouth against the flying bombs; was in the second group of vessels to reach Antwerp in November 1944.

• *Juno*: 21 September 1939 to 19 March 1941: minesweeper, renamed HMS *Helvellyn*, based on the Clyde then at Portland and Milford Haven; moved to the Thames for conversion to an anti-aircraft vessel, hit by a bomb in the Surrey Commercial Docks and sunk on 19 March 1941 while this work was under way.

London & North Eastern Railway

• *Lucy Ashton* remained in service on the Clyde throughout the war years, with only six days out of service.

• *Waverley*: 21 September 1939 to 29 May 1940: minesweeper based at Portsmouth from December 1939, then at Harwich from March 1940; was flotilla leader of the 12th minesweeping flotilla; attempted to tow *Eagle III* off the beach at Dunkirk, but was ordered to return to Dover; half an hour into the voyage at 1700 on 29 May 1940 attacked by a dozen Heinkel aircraft, two of which were claimed to have been brought down by her gunner, hit by three bombs, one of which jammed the rudder and put her steering gear out of action; sank rapidly after three-quarters of an hour; of the 600 troops on board about 300 drowned, and the remainder rescued, many by the buoyant seats which Captain Cameron had insisted be kept in situ when she was being refitted for war service at A. & J. Inglis, and picked up by the French destroyer *Cyclone*, the tug *Java* and the Thames paddle steamer *Golden Eagle*.

• *Marmion*: 21 September 1939 to 9 April 1941; minesweeper based at Portsmouth from December 1939, then at Harwich from March 1940; rescued a total of 745 troops from Dunkirk 29 May to 3 June 1940 in three trips to Dover; sunk by air attack in Harwich Harbour on the night of 8/9 April 1941, raised but she was unfit for further service and scrapped.

• *Jeanie Deans*: 21 September 1939 to June 1945, resumed service 15 May 1946; minesweeper, flagship of the 1st Minesweeping Flotilla based at Irvine, later at Portland and at Milford Haven; converted to an anti-aircraft ship for service on the Thames Estuary during the Blitz from May 8 1941 to July 1941, then used as an escort ship on the east coast between the Tyne and the Humber, and from 1943 based at Harwich as an escort for Trinity House buoying vessels; transferred to the Thames as an anti-aircraft ship against flying bombs, two of which

Jeanie Deans in dazzle camouflage in Govan dry dock preparing for war service in late 1939, showing how her stern had been built up to promenade deck level for this, a feature she retained after the war.

were shot down by her crew; at this time had a race with the Thames paddler *Royal Eagle*, which she won; returned to the Clyde in June 1946.

• *Talisman*: 28 September 1940 to February 1946: renamed HMS *Aristocrat*; fitted with Bofors guns and used as an anti-aircraft vessel; based at Methil, then at Sheerness, sailing to off Margate and towards the Goodwin Sands, also used as a convoy escort vessel in the Thames Estuary nicknamed *Wasp*; used carrying Canadian troops for a precursor to the Dieppe raid, 4–9 July 1942, this was abandoned due to adverse weather; moved to Loch-na-Keal, Mull October 1942 to protect troopships anchored there awaiting orders for the invasion of North Africa, then returned to Sheerness, providing anti-aircraft protection to the Trinity house vessels *Alert* and *Patricia*; used as HQ ship for the first Mulberry Harbour at Arromanches on D-Day, 7 June 1944 until 11 June; continued as anti-aircraft vessel and control vessel for a further five weeks until she was hit in the bow by a landing craft and returned to Portsmouth for repairs; sailed for Harwich, coming under attack off Dover, being shelled and hit in twenty-six places by German guns, but was not seriously damaged; was part of the first convoy to sail up the Scheldt to Antwerp 27 November 1944; used as an escort ship from Antwerp down the Schelde and in convoy protection off the Belgian coast to off Ostend; ran aground in April 1945; repaired at Antwerp, returned to Sheerness on VE Day, 8 May 1945 and used as a ferry from Chatham to Shotley Barracks, Harwich until January 1946, returned to Glasgow February 1946, resumed service 6 July 1946.

Talisman in dazzle camouflage. She was used as an anti-aircraft vessel and escort vessel and her engines performed far better than they had in peacetime.

Williamson Buchanan Steamers (1936) Ltd

• *Kylemore*: 21 July 1939 to 21 August 1940: minesweeper based at Portsmouth, then at Harwich; later used as a net-layer; bombed and sunk off the mouth of the Wash 21 August 1940 while laying nets.

• *Eagle III*: 17 October 1939 to 1945: minesweeper, renamed HMS *Oriole*, based at Portsmouth, later at Harwich; was at Dunkirk 29 May to 4 June, making five trips, one to Harwich and four to Dover, rescuing a total of 2,587 men according to the official figures, but about 5,000 according to a tally kept by her captain; was beached there on her first trip by her captain for 12 hours, with the following signal being sent:

> Deliberately grounded HMS *Oriole* Belgian coast dawn on May 29th on own initiative, objective speedy evacuation of troops. Refloated dusk same day, no apparent damage. Will complete S.232 when operations permit-meantime am again proceeding Belgian Coast and will run aground again if such course seems desirable.

This received the reply 'Your action fully approved.'

She same under heavy aerial attack, and when the tide rose about 2,000 troops waded out to her, crossed her decks and boarded other vessels or small vessels to ferry them to ships anchored offshore on her seaward side; sailed for Dover after she was able to free herself on the rising tide; and returned for another four trips; continued minesweeping until August 1945,

Eagle III on the beach at Dunkirk at low tide. She made five trips there and rescued about 5,000 men.

Eagle III, worn out after war service, being broken up with the Isle of Man Steam Packet's *Snaefell* aft of her.

1 *Dumbuck* of the Dumbarton Steamboat Company, owners from 1847 to 1852. Built in 1832 as *Robert Napier* for service on the Clyde, she ran as *Balloch* on Loch Lomond in summer 1835. The distinctive black-white-black funnel colours of the Dumbarton Steamboat Company can be seen to advantage here.

2 MacBrayne's veteran *Pioneer* (1844) at Corpach. The Oban to Fort William service was extended here to connect with the Caledonian Canal steamer to Inverness prior to the railway being opened to Banavie in 1895.

3 *Iona* (1864) arriving at Ardrishaig with *Columba* already berthed. This is a postcard view, probably from the time after 1903 when *Iona* made a run from Wemyss Bay to Ardrishaig.

4 *Columba* (1878) in the West Kyle of the Kyles of Bute in a postcard view.

5 *Columba* arriving at Gourock in a postcard view. Note the metal 'Caledonian Railway' sign above the pier buildings, a sign that lasted until the 1970s, latterly just saying 'BR'.

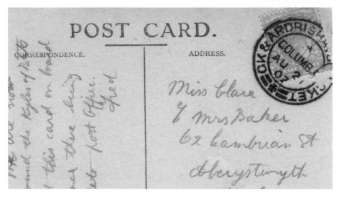

6 *Columba* had her own post office on board, as stated in the message on this card: 'We are now sailing round the Kyles of Bute. I posted this card on board the steamer there being a complete post office on board.' The postmark 'Greenock & Ardrishaig Packet' was used for items posted on the steamer and items bearing this are now highly collectable.

7 A London & North Western Railway official postcard showing *Columba*, *Lord of the Isles* and the CSP's *Marchioness of Breadalbane* at Rothesay Pier in the early years of the twentieth century.

8 *Empress* (1888) lying stationary on Loch Lomond.

9 An official Caledonian Railway postcard showing *Duchess of Hamilton* in a stormy sea. The black and white version of this photo was on display in the dining room of the turbine *Duchess of Hamilton* in the 1960s. Posted in 1905, the message on the reverse of the card states '... sailing round Arran and Ailsa. Rough & Wet...'.

10 *Lord of the Isles* (1891) in a postcard view after her promenade deck was extended forwards in 1898.

11 The reverse of the above card showing the steamer's own cachet, posted on 14 July 1910 with the message, 'Having a lovely sail. All enjoying ourselves, Aunt Jeanette.'

12 The GSWR's *Neptune* arriving at Ayr in a postcard view.

13 A postcard issued onboard the GSWR's *Mercury* (1892) where the central portion can be lifted to reveal a concertina of views of the Firth of Clyde.

14 *Princess May* at Tarbet Pier, Loch Lomond in a postcard view with a Rob Roy tartan surround.

15 The GSWR's *Juno* of 1898 depicted on an official postcard.

16 *Duchess of Fife* (1903) at Rothesay pier in an early colour photo from the late 1940s or early 1950s.

17 *Jeanie Deans* (1931) being warped round in the River Clyde off Bridge Wharf.

18 *Jeanie Deans* at Tighnabruaich in 1964.

19 *Caledonia* (1934) arriving at Gourock in 1969, probably from Craigendoran.

20 *Caledonia* at Tarbert, Loch Fyne in 1969.

21 An official postcard from *Mercury* (1934).

22 *Talisman* (1935) at Tighnabruaich in 1965 or 1966.

23 *Waverley* passing the Erskine Bridge under construction in 1970.

24 *Waverley* in the Kyles of Bute in 1969.

25 *Waverley* at Lochgoilhead in 1964, the final year the pier was open.

26 *Waverley* at Arrochar in 1964 with passengers disembarking, many for the Three Lochs Tour, to walk the mile and a half, or take a bus, to Tarbet on Loch Lomond.

27 *Waverley* at anchor in Loch Riddon, 1972, on charter to the Paddle Steamer Preservation Society, making a call by tender at Ormidale.

28 *Waverley* at Lamont's berth, Port Glasgow, taken from Newark Castle, with her forward funnel in a trial red-yellow-black livery for 1973, her first season under Caledonian MacBrayne, one that was quickly replaced by the standard CalMac funnel.

29 *Waverley* in the East India Harbour, Greenock, awaiting the start of the season in 1973, now in full CalMac colours.

30 *Waverley* departing Dunoon in 1973, the only year in which she was in service with CalMac colours.

31 *Waverley* in Lamont's dry dock being surveyed after her sale to Waverley Steam Navigation Co. in 1974.

32 *Waverley* arriving at Ayr at speed, 1975.

33 *Waverley* about to enter Griffin Dock, Ayr, 1975.

34 *Waverley* at speed in Rothesay Bay, 1994.

35 *Maid of the Loch* in her present livery at Balloch Pier, taken from Drumkinnon Tower, awaiting re-awakening in her fortieth year in 1993.

36 The final Clyde paddle steamer to be built, the 1962 replica of Henry Bell's *Comet*, on her maiden voyage surrounded by yachts and pilot boats and Clyde Marine Motoring's vessels.

37 *Jeanie Deans* (1931) taken in 1963.

38 *Waverley* (1947) arriving at Gourock in 1970 or 1971.

39 The Clyde paddle steamer entered the folklore of the West of Scotland, as seen here in an image of the GSWR's *Neptune* in tiles on the wall of a close in Greenock dating from 1900.

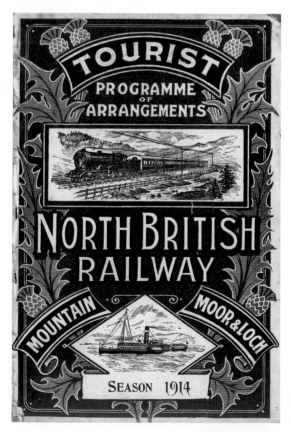

40 The cover of a North British Railway Tourist Programme for 1914 with a drawing of *Marmion*.

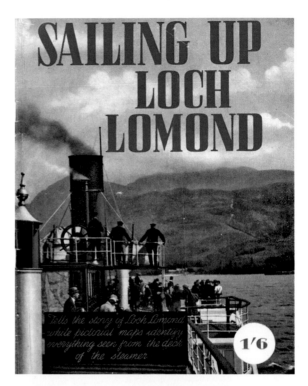

41 A deck view on *Prince Edward* or *Princess May* in a guide booklet published around 1946.

42 The front cover of the 1901 GSWR timetable, showing a stylised map of the Firth of Clyde and the company's routes.

43 *Marion* (1817), the first steamer on Loch Lomond.

44 *Eagle* (1852) in two-funnelled condition prior to 1860.

45 The cover of the Caledonian Steam Packet 1905 timetable.

46 The cover of a MacBrayne timetable from the early 1900s showing *Columba*.

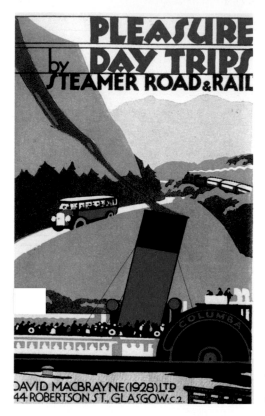

47 The cover of a MacBrayne timetable from 1928, still showing *Columba*, but with echoes of art deco design.

48 The *Waverley* keeps the Clyde paddle steamer tradition alive.

when she was used as a relief ship with supplies for the Netherlands; returned to the Clyde and laid up in the Holy Loch, by then her haystack boiler was worn out and was too expensive to replace; sold for scrapping at Smith & Houston, Port Glasgow, 17 August 1946.

• *Queen Empress*: 17 October 1939 to 1944; minesweeper based at Portsmouth, flagship of the 12th Minesweeping Flotilla, later at Harwich; shot down two German aircraft in May and September 1943 respectively; continued minesweeping until August 1945, when she was used as a relief ship with supplies for the Netherlands; worn out and sold to a firm in the Netherlands for scrapping 5 August 1946.

David MacBrayne Ltd

In 1939 MacBrayne only had two remaining paddle steamers:

• *Gondolier*: June 1940: By this time 73 years old, *Gondolier* would probably soon have gone to the breakers if not for the war. Taken over by the Admiralty in June 1940, her engines, boiler, sponsons, paddle boxes and saloons were removed at Inverness and she was towed north to be sunk as a blockship at Scapa Flow.

• *Pioneer*: 21 March 1944 until 1958: used as the HQ of submarine control for the North Atlantic, stationed off Fairlie, later used as a research ship for the Department of Submarine Warfare, renamed HMS *Harbinger* in 1945; converted January 1946 for use as a floating laboratory in Portland Harbour until scrapped in March 1958.

The War Years on the Firth

The war years from 1914–18 and 1939–45 proved a telling time in the Firth. The estuary became a hive of naval activity during both wars, and a boom erected from the Cloch to Dunoon meant that many services had to be altered, e.g. MacBrayne's Royal Route service to Tarbert and Ardrishaig started from Wemyss Bay. Many services were butchered to become the short routes we know today. With only a few exceptions the paddle steamers were taken up by the Admiralty and casualties were to be expected. The design of paddle steamers made them ideal for use as minesweepers, and as anti-aircraft vessels. Throughout, they covered themselves in glory in far-flung parts of the UK and Europe. The Dunkirk Evacuation in May 1940 (Operation Dynamo) proved their worth and at the D-Day Normandy Landings in June 1944, the Admiralty were fulsome in praise of them.

The 1899 *Waverley* and her master John Cameron became legends as the Dunkirk story unfolded and the 1947 *Waverley* in preservation made much of it in the 1980 and 1990 anniversaries. In 2010, John's widow Jean sailed 'doon the watter' to Arrochar in October on *Waverley*. Although not part of the official ceremony, Mrs Cameron paid her own private tribute to John and the brave souls of those momentous days in May and June 1940. John became master of the 1947 *Waverley*, retired in 1970 and died in 1989, having told the story many times of the Hell of Dunkirk.

The story of the Clyde steamers at war could fill a book in itself, but for sure all of them did a large part in the war effort, to bring peace to our country and continent.

Lucy Ashton in 1945 in yellow ochre war paint.

Marchioness of Lorne in a lighter overall paint condition leaving Hunter's Quay.

Post War Retrenchment

On return to the Clyde in 1946 after war service, three steamers were felt to be too worn out to be reconditioned and were scrapped. These were *Eagle III* and *Queen-Empress* from the erstwhile Williamson-Buchanan fleet, and *Duchess of Rothesay* from the CSP fleet. The final pre-1914 paddlers were withdrawn and scrapped in the next few years: the veteran ex-NB *Lucy Ashton* in 1949, *Duchess of Fife* in 1953 and, on Loch Lomond, *Princess May* in 1953 and *Prince Edward* in 1955. *Jupiter* was withdrawn after the 1957 season, only a year after conversion to oil-firing, leaving only four paddlers to survive into the 1960s for the 150th Anniversary of the *Comet*. A replica of the 1812 *Comet* was constructed for this anniversary, but was never in public service, only making a couple of trips from Greenock to Helensburgh with VIPs, and later being placed on display on land in Port Glasgow, where she remains to this day. Of the remaining paddlers, *Jeanie Deans* was withdrawn after the 1964 season, *Talisman* in early 1967 and *Caledonia* in 1969, after a brief period relieving on MacBrayne's Tarbert mail service, leaving only *Waverley* in service on the Clyde and *Maid of the Loch* on Loch Lomond, the latter continuing in service until 1981. By then her owners, Caledonian MacBrayne, were in the business of providing car ferry services rather than pleasure cruises.

The post-war period was a story of decline, withdrawals, and scrappings as the old steamers were replaced by the car ferry, a soulless type of craft with a duty to perform. The expansion of private motoring and road improvements in the Highlands and Islands meant that passengers and goods could reach the resorts of the Clyde Coast and the islands of the Hebrides much quicker and more conveniently using car ferries than by paddle steamer. Beauties they are not and in comparison to the crackers of paddle steamers our fine estuary has boasted over the past 200 years, they deserve little mention in this volume. As for the *Comet* and its links, 200 years later we must be proud of the present *Waverley*, without whom this volume would have no place and this history would have ended almost forty years ago.

As you sail down the Clyde, look out for Henry Bell's monument at Dunglass, just downstream from Bowling, and acknowledge the man who gave us the Clyde steamers and as a thump of the paddles echoes across, surely Bell is happy with that as all on board *Waverley* continue 'in the wake of the *Comet*.'

The paddle box of *Duchess of Fife*, seen in her penultimate season in 1952.

Jupiter off Gourock in the 1950s.

Caledonia off Bridge Wharf in summer 1964.

Princess May on Loch Lomond in 1949–52 colours with a black hull.

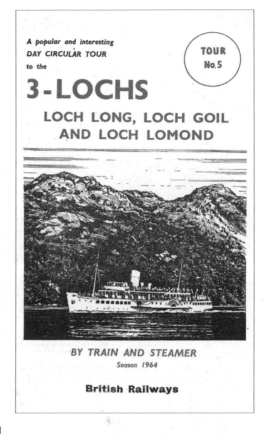

Above left: The cover of the 1955 Loch Lomond
timetable with the then almost new *Maid of the Loch*.

Above right: A handbill for the Three Lochs cruise for the 1964 season, featuring a drawing of *Maid of*

A handbill for Caledonian Steam Packet services from Kilcreggan
in 1970, incongruously with a drawing of *Maid of the Loch*. The
Three Lochs Tour is mentioned towards the bottom of the page,
however.

Waverley off Dunoon in 1948 with brown deck saloons.

Waverley off Gourock in the mid-1950s, now with white deck saloons.

Waverley in the mid-1950s off Brodick.

Waverley departing Gourock in 1959, now with white paddle boxes.

The Preservation Era

In November 1965 the former LNER paddle steamer *Jeanie Deans* left the Firth for the Thames under the flag of the Coastal Steam Packet Co., a very clever flag as it was the old LNER Scottish saltire but with CSPCo. rather than LNER, one letter in each blue segment.

The concept of preservation had started with this venture that sadly would be so dogged with a variety of breakdowns that it was to end in sadness mid-way through the 1967 season.

Jeanie Deans preserved – what a lovely idea! Renamed *Queen of the South*, a great name! Even better was her livery, back to the red, white and black funnel. Attractive publicity was superb and a team of very enthusiastic personnel was employed but machinery- and boiler-wise she was a bit past her best and a lot of paddle trouble marred her two seasons of 1966 and 1967. The addition of a bow rudder and guards at the base of each paddle box to deflect floating debris helped a bit. The whole idea of *Queen of the South* was a wonderful thought but failed only because of her poor mechanical performance. As *Queen of the South* she utilised all available piers on the Thames estuary: Tower Pier, Greenwich, Tilbury, Southend, and Herne Bay and made Thames Estuary cruises. On her voyage south in 1965 with red, yellow and black funnels she called at Stranraer, Falmouth, Southampton and Tilbury, where she berthed with the veteran motor vessel *Anzio I*, formerly MacBrayne's *Lochinvar*.

Caledonia headed south in 1971 to become what was possibly the UK's first floating pub. After work at Lamont's Port Glasgow yard, including the removal of her masts and the top of her funnel, she made for the Thames under tow. She opened in 1972, moored at Hungerford Bridge as *Old Caledonia*, and was tastefully looked after with some acknowledgement of her history and was successful until destroyed by fire on 27 April 1980. Later broken up at Grays in Essex, her engines have survived and are now on display at the Hollycombe Collection at Liphook in Hampshire, where they are occasionally operated using steam from a portable boiler.

Maid of the Loch was withdrawn in 1981 and has been laid up at Balloch Pier ever since. The PSPS Scottish Branch initially, and now the Loch Lomond Steamship Company, have looked after the *Maid*, trying her out as a static venue. They have restored the winch house and steam slipway adjacent to the pier, which will be ideal for out-of-the-water surveys. At times in the year this is in full steam and worth a visit. At the time of writing a major appeal for funds is planned in an attempt to raise enough money for a new boiler in 2013 and a return to operation in 2014. It would be good to see the paddles turn again.

Waverley: the story of this world-famous Clyde steamer has been often told, so all that needs to be said is that she is the last sea-going paddle steamer in the world and operates

Bowling was for many years the favoured winter lay-up berth for many Clyde steamers, as seen here in this image from 1920s with *Fusilier*, *Waverley* and *Columba* in the front row, with *Iona* and at least another five steamers behind in a veritable forest of funnels.

Waverley and *Caledonia* berthed in Rothesay Dock in the winter of 1969/70.

Glen Sannox in GSWR colours on the slipway at Blackwood & Gordon's yard at Port Glasgow.

Columba in dry dock at Govan prior to her final season in 1935.

public cruises every year. She is powered by a 2,100 hp triple expansion steam engine and has been fully restored to her as-built livery from 1947 and has been tastefully upgraded with twenty-first-century facilities in keeping as much as possible as it would have been in 1947. The attention to detail in her two-phase rebuild in 2000 and 2003 has been exemplary.

She is a must-do trip and is a classic link to 1812 and Henry Bell's *Comet* as she operates on the Clyde and at times on Bell's original route from Glasgow to Greenock and Helensburgh, and to all the remaining ports and piers of the glorious Firth of Clyde and, for a week or so in May or June each year, in the waters frequented by MacBrayne's paddle steamers in the West Highlands out of Oban.

The preservation of vessels like *Waverley* in operational condition is without doubt the best way to preserve a paddle steamer. Sadly, few ventures have made it and although *Waverley* has steamed through tough times, 37 years is a huge milestone. Thanks to the will and determination of a few dedicated enthusiasts, many happy passengers have enjoyed the thrill of going to sea in a paddle steamer. The idea of *Waverley* motionless and moored up never to sail again is surely the very last resort.

We must acknowledge all those who worked ceaselessly to get her into service in 1975 and have kept this piece of living heritage steaming on for the past thirty-seven seasons and onwards to the feature.

Relics

There are a number of relics of long-gone paddle steamers still in existence:

• The deckhouse from the 1864 *Iona* was owned by A. B. Murdoch of Giffnock until his death in 1983. It was auctioned some years ago by the PSPS but its present location is unknown.
• The deckhouse over the forward companionway of the *Lucy Ashton* was owned by Graham Langmuir until his death in 1994 and is now in the Scottish Maritime Museum at Irvine.
• One paddle box carving from *Lucy Ashton* showing Lucy Ashton is in the National Railway Museum, York.
• The ship's wheel from *Lucy Ashton* is in the vestibule of Hermitage Academy at Craigendoran.
• The whistle from MacBrayne's *Columba* is in the PSPS collection. Its present whereabouts is unknown.
• The name from the paddle box from *Jeanie Deans* of 1931 was on display in the forward bar of *Waverley* for many years until about the time of the rebuild. Its present whereabouts is unknown.
• The original 1947 boiler from *Waverley* was donated in 1981 to the Scottish Railway Preservation Society, who had it on display at Bo'ness for a number of years. It is now at the Scottish Maritime Museum at Irvine.
• A deckhouse of the 1903 *Duchess of Fife* was salvaged from the shipbreakers when she was broken up in 1953 by a private individual but was destroyed many years later. Her paddle box crest is in Bute Museum, Rothesay.
• Various bells and crests are the property of Glasgow City Council, and some were displayed in the Clyde room of the Museum of Transport when it was at the Kelvin Hall.
• The paddle box decorations of *Caledonia* of 1899, *Duchess of Hamilton* of 1890 and *Marchioness of Lorne* of 1891 were in display for many years at Gourock and Wemyss Bay stations respectively, until the late 1970s, but their present whereabouts are unknown.
• The present *Waverley*'s whistle was originally on *Eagle III*, and is still in working order today.
• The mast of the 1891 *Marchioness of Lorne* became a well-known flagpole within the playing fields of Glasgow High School in Anniesland for many years until destroyed in the early 1980s.
• A porthole from the 1899 *Waverley* was presented to Glasgow Museums by Mrs Cameron, widow of Captain J. E. Cameron, DSC in 1989.
• *Waverley*'s 1972 and 1996 masts were cut up and sold as souvenirs to raise funds for her rebuild in 2000 and 2003 respectively.

Lord of the Isles being scrapped at Smith & Co., later Smith & Houston, at Port Glasgow in 1928.

The end of the greatest; demolishing the paddle box of *Columba* in 1936 at Arnott Young's at Dalmuir.

The 1961 and 1962 funnels of *Waverley* were disposed of in Norwich on removal from the steamer during her 2000 rebuild at Great Yarmouth. The 'Clyde Built' annexe of the Scottish Maritime Museum at Braehead Shopping Centre refused to accept them.

The Clyde River Steamer Club

Eighty years ago a small band of like-minded enthusiasts formed this club in June 1932. Initially a letter in a Glasgow newspaper brought about its formation and at its peak it reached 750 members. Meetings were, and still are, held in Glasgow in the winter months, currently in Jury's Hotel in Jamaica Street, and an annual magazine with historical articles and an annual review covering all Scottish passenger-carrying vessels are published.

Charters of vessels, both large and small, have made sailings to unusual ports of call possible. Paddle steamers used have been *Lucy Ashton* in her final season of 1948, *Caledonia* in the 1960s, *Waverley* from the 1960s until the present day and *Maid of the Loch*. Sadly the glory days of the paddle steamer have gone, but many former favourites have been remembered during these trips. Waverley Excursions, the present *Waverley* operators, have also commemorated old ships with special sailings, often re-enacting routes and cruises of the past. For more information on the Clyde River Steamer Club, go to www.crsc.org.uk. Membership is normally £23 a year, but new members have a special offer of just £10 for the first year.

Subscriptions should be sent to Stuart Craig, 50 Earlspark Avenue, Newlands, Glasgow, G43 2HW

The West Highland Steamer Club

Want to find out more about the paddle steamers of the West Highlands?
Join the **West Highland Steamer Club**
Introductory Offer: **Only £10** for first year's subscription

Two journals a year with the tiniest details of the various CalMac ships' movements and occasional articles on long-gone steamers.

Meetings in Glasgow monthly from October until April

Please send subscriptions to the treasurer:
Robin Love, 29 Cyprus Ave, Elderslie, Renfrewshire, PA5 8NB

PART 2

21 SIGNIFICANT STEAMERS

Iona (1864)

Iona was built in 1864 by J. & G. Thomson at Govan, before they moved to Clydebank, for David Hutcheson & Co. for the Royal Route from Glasgow to Ardrishaig, connecting with, from 1866, *Linnet* on the Crinan Canal, which connected at Crinan with *Chevalier* for Oban, Fort William and Corpach and onward connections to Inverness. She inherited her deck saloons from her predecessor of the same name, which had been sold for blockade running after only one season, and these were not carried to the edge of the hull as in later steamers such as *Columba*.

She originally had short funnels, which were lengthened and moved closer together on her second reboilering in 1891. The bridge over her paddle boxes was not added until the winter of 1870/71 and Chadburn telegraphs and steam steering gear were added in 1873. The MacBrayne Centenary booklet of 1951 claims that the latter was the first such unit to be fitted to a steamer anywhere in the world. From 1879 her owner became David MacBrayne, this becoming a limited company in 1905.

From 1864 until 1877 she operated in the summer months to Ardrishaig, and on the arrival of *Columba* in 1878 she gave an additional sailing on the route. From 1880 to 1885 she was based at Oban and operated the Crinan to Corpach run and in 1886 was back on the Ardrishaig service, leaving there in the morning and returning from the Broomielaw at 13:30. From 1903 she departed Ardrishaig at 05:45 for Wemyss Bay, making a non-stop trip back from there to arrive at Ardrishaig at around the same time as *Columba*, and then making an afternoon run to Wemyss Bay and back. Winter lay up was at Bowling until 1928, and thenceforth at Greenock.

She had new boilers fitted in 1875, and again in 1891, at which time a surface condenser replaced the original jet one. Her two-cylinder simple oscillating engine served her throughout her 72 years.

She remained on the Clyde during the First World War, painted an all-over grey, and from August 1916 she was chartered by the Caledonian Steam Packet Co., mainly operating from Wemyss Bay to Rothesay. For a short period she was painted with their yellow funnel.

After the war she was on the Lochgoilhead and Arrochar service until 1927, after which she ran from Oban to Fort William with seasonal reliefs on the Ardrishaig service. With the remainder of the fleet, ownership was transferred to David MacBrayne (1928) Ltd after the reorganisation in 1928.

She was withdrawn from service after the 1935 season and was towed to Dalmuir to be broken up by the tugs *Vanguard* and *Cruiser* on 27 February 1936. Thus ended the remarkable cumulative total of 129 years service of *Iona* and *Columba* on the Firth.

Opposite: Iona (1864) departing Dunoon.

Columba (1878)

Columba was built by J. & G. Thomson at Clydebank for David Hutcheson & Co., and launched on 11 April 1878, being the final steamer built for that company, which was taken over by David MacBrayne in the following year. At 301.4 feet she was to be the longest Clyde steamer ever built. She had an innovative steel hull and two cylinder oscillating engines, but these were never converted to compound. Originally fitted with four navy boilers, these were replaced by two haystack boilers in 1900. She differed from her predecessor on the route, *Iona*, in that her saloons were carried out to the edge of the hull. She was built to counter opposition from the first *Lord of the Isles*, which called at most MacBrayne Ardrishaig route calling points en route to Inveraray.

She served all her life as the summer steamer on the Royal Route from Glasgow to Ardrishaig. She initially left Glasgow at 7 a.m., later changed to 7:11, and stood out among any sailing list. She was a very cumbersome ship to handle, with most unusual manoeuvres such as coaling being done in the evening and very early morning. She steamed up to Bridge Wharf north and later south side stern first, then headed off to coal at General Terminus, then back up river stern first among dozens of coastal ships, a manoeuvre not for the faint hearted.

Her funnels were lengthened in spring 1884, new funnels were fitted at the reboilering in 1900, a companionway cover was added in 1901, and a smoke room aft of the companionway added some time in the early years of the twentieth century, with an upper deck and two lifeboats added above that in 1914 to meet post-*Titanic* regulations, but generally her appearance altered little over her career.

On board facilities included a post office (until 1914), a hairdressing salon, a fruit stall and a bookstall. Her passenger clientele in First Class included many moneyed people travelling north to their shooting lodges in the West Highlands.

During the First World War she was laid up in 1915 and ran from Wemyss Bay rather than Glasgow from August 1916 until the end of the 1918 season because of the boom which had ben erected between the Cloch and Dunoon.

In 1929 the hull and paddle boxes were painted grey but reverted to black after a couple of weeks.

A splendid guide book was issued, fully illustrated and now much sought after, which featured all the company's routes, with *Columba* on the cover, in gilt on the hardback edition, and was published annually up to about 1914. She still featured on the covers of the company's timetables until the advent of the motor vessels in the early 1930s.

Columba was withdrawn after the 1935 summer season and was sold in April 1936 to Arnott Young & Co. (Shipbreakers) Ltd and broken up at Dalmuir, brining much sadness on the Firth and the river.

Both *Columba* and *Iona* were replaced in 1936 by the turbine steamer *Saint Columba* on the Ardrishaig run, her name appropriately perpetuating that of her predecessor.

Opposite: Columba (1878).

Ivanhoe (1880)

Ivanhoe was built in 1880 at the yard of D. & W. Henderson at Meadowside for the Frith (sic) of Clyde Steam Packet Co. This was syndicate of Alexander Allan, of the Allan Line, George Smith, Captain James Brown of the City Line and three others with Captain James Williamson the captain of the steamer, which was run on teetotal principles. She had two-cylinder, non-compound diagonal oscillating engines.

She made a trip under charter from Glasgow to the Gareloch and Loch Goil prior to entering service. On 1 May 1880 her maiden voyage took her from Helensburgh and both Greenock Piers, Custom House Quay and Albert Harbour, as the station that became Princes Pier was known prior to the completion of the new pier in 1894, to Corrie, Brodick and Lamlash via the Kyles of Bute. Cruises round Arran, to Ailsa Craig and to Campbeltown Loch, also featured in her programme. From the opening of Craigendoran Pier in 1882, the sailings commenced from there, and from the year prior to the opening of Gourock Pier in 1888 it was served rather than the two piers at Greenock. She was reboilered in 1892.

In spring 1892 she spent a spell on the Manchester Ship Canal, commencing service on 23 March with a single journey each way from Liverpool to Manchester in one or other direction, as offered today by Mersey Ferries. On 22 May 1894 she completed this duty with a trip from Manchester to Liverpool and returned to the Clyde.

The Frith of Clyde Steam Packet Co. ceased business on 28 April 1897 and she was sold to the Caledonian Steam Packet Co. Ltd, of which James Williamson was the Manager and Secretary. A bar was added and her paddle boxes were painted white. She operated in that year on rail-connected services from Gourock to the main Clyde resorts and from the following year on cruises including Arrochar, Millport, round Arran and 'Round the Lochs'. In 1906 she was on a service from Gourock to Tighnabruaich then was laid up until 1911.

In 1911 she was sold to the Firth of Clyde Steam Packet Co. Ltd and her funnels painted white and her paddle boxes black. She was used for cruises from Glasgow to Rothesay. On 10 May 1914 she followed the new Cunard liner *Aquitania* down river.

In June 1914 she was acquired by Turbine Steamers Ltd and in that summer operated from Glasgow to Lochgoilhead as a replacement for the scrapped *Edinburgh Castle*. Her funnels received thin black tops, which were deepened in 1916. She was chartered by the Caledonian Steam Packet from 1917 to 1919 to replace steamers which had been called up for war service. Laid up in 1919, she was towed to Dumbarton and scrapped on 14 September 1920.

The name Firth of Clyde Steam Packet Co. Ltd was resurrected in 1980 for the company which owned the motor vessel *Shanklin*, which was renamed *Prince Ivanhoe* and was lost off the Gower coast in South Wales in August 1981.

Opposite: Ivanhoe (1880) between 1912 and 1914, with thin black tops on her funnels.

Grenadier (1885)

Grenadier, known in some quarters as 'Grannie dear', was built in 1885 at J. & G. Thomson's yard at Clydebank for David MacBrayne, and was beautifully turned out with a clipper bow and bowsprit. She was intended to sail from Oban to Mull, Skye and Gairloch, but after only a year she was moved to the Staffa and Iona 'Sacred Isle' cruise round Mull from Oban, which she maintained from June to September almost without exception until 1927. She was normally on the Glasgow to Ardrishaig run in the winter months. She had the first compound engine of the diagonal oscillating type fitted to a Clyde or West Highland paddle steamer. In early 1889 she was involved in an incident with the schooner *Lady Margaret* at Colintraive. The latter was discharging lime at the pier and pulled off to allow *Grenadier* to call. As the steamer approached, a gust of wind pushed the schooner towards the steamer, which struck her jib boom with her paddle box and felled her mast, which fell across *Grenadier*'s deck, striking a group of passengers, killing one and severely injuring another. It was very unusual for a passenger to lose their life on board a Clyde paddle steamer.

In 1902 she was re-boilered when two haystack boilers replaced the original navy boilers, along with larger diameter funnels, and was a very handsome steamer in this condition. In the summer of 1902 she was on the Clyde, running to Rothesay and Tighnabruaich from Glasgow. In 1915 and the early part of 1916, she ran from Wemyss Bay to Ardrishaig because of the boom from the Cloch to Dunoon.

In the 1914–18 war she served as HMS *Grenade* as a minesweeper in the North Sea from 3 July 1916 to 23 October 1919.

On 5 September 1927 she caught fire while berthed overnight at Oban North Pier, with the loss of three lives, including Captain Macarthur, who had retired after the previous summer but who had continued as an 'advisor' to the new captain, and who was sleeping on board at the time. She was badly damaged and was towed to Ardrossan on 11 May 1928 to be broken up. Her boilers were recycled, with one going to *Gondolier* and the other to *Glencoe*. Again it has to be said that *Grenadier* was exceptionally attractive and must have brought great colour to any scene.

Opposite: Grenadier (1886) going astern out of Oban in her later years with large funnels, post-1913 with more lifeboats.

Victoria (1886)

Victoria was built in 1886 by Blackwood & Gordon at Port Glasgow for Gillies & Campbell and was the first Clyde steamer to be fitted with electric light. She had 160 hp, two-cylinder diagonal engines and operated in connection with Caledonian Railway trains from Wemyss Bay but was frequently used for her owners' cruising duties.

She was in demand as the Club Steamer for the Clyde yacht racing fortnight until *Duchess of Hamilton* appeared in 1890. The Caledonian Railway connection ceased in 1889 and she ran on Belfast Lough under charter in competition with Moore Bros vessels, and made one trip from Liverpool to Llandudno in May 1890.

She was sold in 1891 to Morris Carsewell and his Scottish Excursion Steamer Co. Ltd and was chartered by Gunning Naerup le Boulanger of Swansea, running to Ilfracombe from 29 July 1891. The venture was unsuccessful and her last sail there was on 29 August 1891.

She was refurbished and reboilered by her builders and from 24 June 1892 opened a service from Greenock to Campbeltown. In the following year she ran in connection with the Glasgow & South Western Railway thrice weekly from Greenock Princes Pier and Fairlie to Campbeltown, with excursions on the other days to Ailsa Craig, Ayr and Culzean Bay and from Glasgow to the Kyles of Bute. On 17 September 1893 fire broke out while she was lying at the Broomielaw. It was extinguished after two hours and did £3,000 worth of damage.

In 1895 she passed to the London & East Coast Express Steamship Service Ltd and ran out of London, but returned to the Firth in 1897, owned by Clyde Steamers Ltd (Andrew Dawson Reid) and sailing from Glasgow, including the aforementioned Sunday trips to Dunoon. She was broken up in the Netherlands in September 1900. Victoria was a steamer that never realised her potential, only sailing on the Firth for a total of seven seasons.

Opposite: Victoria (1886) departing Craigmore.

Lucy Ashton (1888)

Lucy Ashton was built in 1888 by T. B. Seath & Co. of Rutherglen with a single cylinder diagonal engine by Hutson & Corbett and was launched on 24 May 1888 by Miss Darling, daughter of her owners' Secretary and Manager, for the North British Steam Packet Co. Ltd for service from Craigendoran. Initially she ran to the Holy Loch piers and in 1895, on the appearance of *Dandie Dinmont*, she became spare and was used on excursions and charters. From 1909 she moved to the Gareloch service, a route which she remained on until 1938. A purser's office was added in 1894 with a new bridge above it. In 1901 she received a new boiler and in the following year, after her connecting rod had broken, A. & J. Inglis provided new engines of the two-cylinder compound type, a decision that ensured her longevity, and another new boiler, her year-old boiler going to *Lady Rowena*. The following year the deck saloons were extended to give greater covered accommodation, although the fore saloon was not extended to the edge of the hull, and in 1908 companionway shelters were added on the promenade deck above the stairs to the fore-saloon and a new captain's cabin and purser's office and deck shelter were added aft of the funnel on the promenade deck. In 1902 ownership was transferred to the North British Railway. She remained on the Firth throughout the 1914–18 war, although not sailing south of Dunoon because of the boom. The new steamer *Fair Maid* of 1915 was built to replace her but did not survive war service. Another new boiler was fitted in late 1922, and in 1923, with the railway amalgamation, she became owned by the London & North Eastern Railway.

With the remainder of the LNER fleet, her hull and paddle boxes were painted grey in 1936. She was laid up in 1939 until recalled to service after *Talisman* broke down, and served on the Clyde throughout the Second World War, running to Gourock instead of Greenock Princes Pier, and Dunoon and was painted grey all over with the pennant number D56 on her bow. In May 1945 her funnel was painted back to the red, white and black of the LNER and she was painted in the pre-1936 hull colours in 1946. Railway nationalisation in 1948 saw her funnel painted yellow with a black top on 23 February of that year. She remained in service until February 1949, by which time she was the final nineteenth-century steamer in service on the Firth and the last one with a bridge aft of the funnel. She was used on 29 May 1948 for the first 'big-ship' charter by the Clyde River Steamer Club, visiting many of the piers she had known so well over the past 60 years, a fitting swansong to her career. A train hauled by the locomotive *Lucy Ashton* brought the passengers from Glasgow (Queen St High Level) to Craigendoran for the trip.

She was sold on 29 November 1949 to Metal Industries (Salvage) Ltd and reduced to main deck level, then sold on to the British Shipbuilding Research Association and fitted with four Rolls-Royce jet engines and used for hull resistance tests in the Gareloch, cruising at 20 knots. 'A Rolls-Royce *Lucy*' was broken up at Faslane in December 1951. She had ended service as one of the most popular paddlers of all time.

Opposite: Lucy Ashton (1888).

Duchess of Hamilton (1890)

Duchess of Hamilton was built in 1890 by William Denny & Bros of Dumbarton for the Caledonian Steam Packet Co. Ltd. She had two-crank compound engines and her promenade deck was extended to the bow, being the first Clyde paddle steamer to have this feature. A mean speed of 18.1 knots was achieved on trials on 28 May 1890 and she opened the new service from Ardrossan (Montgomerie Pier) to the east Arran piers of Brodick, Whiting Bay and Lamlash on 30 May 1890 in competition with Captain Buchanan's *Scotia*, operating in connection with the GSWR. In addition, she served as the club steamer for the Royal Clyde Yacht Club's annual fortnight. From 1892 *Glen Sannox* was in completion with her on the Arran service, and could put up more of a fight than the aging *Scotia*.

In 1906 the new turbine steamer *Duchess of Argyll* succeeded her on the Arran route and from then on she was based at Gourock. New boilers were installed later in 1906. She inaugurated Sunday sailings to Dunoon and Rothesay on 6 June 1909.

She had spells of cruising on the Firth, from Ayr in 1898 and from Gourock in 1906, and to Arran via the Kyles in 1909. From 1910 she was on general excursion work and also did the Arrochar run from Gourock.

In February 1915 she was requisitioned by the Admiralty and was initially on transport services from Southampton to France. In September of that year she was converted to a minesweeper and struck a mine and sank near Harwich on 29 November 1915.

She was the prototype for the *Belle* paddle fleet on the Thames and her hull was duplicated in 1901 for the turbine *King Edward*, where provision was made to convert the latter to a paddle steamer should the new turbine propulsion not be satisfactory.

Opposite: Duchess of Hamilton (1890) in an official Caledonian Railway postcard view. Posted in Rothesay in August 1908, the message on the reverse states 'The *Duchess of Hamilton* has taken us on some fine trips from here. The Scotch Rlys have to use steamers largely as well as trains. It seems strange never to hears a loco's whistle here on Bute'.

Lord of the Isles (1891)

The second *Lord of the Isles* was built in 1891 by D. & W. Henderson at Partick. She was similar to her predecessor of the same name, but her saloons were extended right to the edge of the hull. She had similar two-cylinder diagonal oscillating machinery, and was about 11 feet longer. She was placed on the long all-day trip from Glasgow to Inveraray and was owned by the Glasgow & Inveraray Steamboat Co., which was managed by Malcolm T. Clark, who also managed the Lochgoil Company. In 1898 her promenade deck was extended to the bow, the condition in which she is seen in the majority of photographs and postcards.

In 1909 her owners merged with the Lochgoil Company to form the Lochgoil & Inveraray Steamboat Co. From 1903 she had competition on the route with the turbine steamer *King Edward* and in 1912 was taken over by Turbine Steamers Ltd, although she retained her funnel markings. From 1912 she sailed on excursions from Glasgow round Bute.

She remained on the Clyde during the 1914–18 war, mainly sailing to Lochgoilhead. In 1928 she was moved to the Glasgow to Lochgoilhead and Arrochar service to replace *Iona*, which had moved up to Oban, and these sailings were advertised by MacBraynes, and in spring of that year she had a short spell on the Ardrishaig mail service. At the end of that year she was sold to Smith & Houston in Port Glasgow for £1,000 for breaking up. She was the last steamer on the Clyde to have polished copper steam pipes, which were attached to her funnels.

Opposite: Lord of the Isles (1891) with the 1902 turbine *Queen Alexandra* in the background.

Glen Sannox (1892)

Built in 1892 purely for the service from Ardrossan to Arran, there can be no doubt that the name of *Glen Sannox* was one of the finest ever bestowed on a Clyde paddle steamer. With the majestic two-funnelled paddler came speed and comfort and she was a match for all other steamers, even the turbines, which were given a run at races at times, albeit at a high price in coal consumption. She had compound diagonal engines and reached 19.23 knots on trials. She was the first Clyde paddle steamer to have the promenade deck extended up to the bow and plated in below that.

She served the three east Arran piers of Brodick, Lamlash and Whiting Bay with a ferry call at Kings Cross, and at Whiting Bay prior to the completion of the pier there in 1899. Initially she offered cruises from the Arran ports during her midday layover time between her arrival at Whiting Bay at 11:15 and her return sailing at 15:10, round Arran, round Ailsa Craig and to Campbeltown Loch on different days of the week, but in later years made a return trip to Ardrossan during that period. Following the pooling arrangement with the CSP in 1908 she was laid up in 1910 and was on the run to Arran via the Kyles in 1912.

In 1915 she was taken up by the Admiralty and sent to Southampton with the intention of being used as a troopship to Le Havre. She was there for a month, and was then returned to her owners and to the Arran service, partly because her hull was too light for the rigorous cross-Channel service and partly because of her high coal consumption. She continued on the Arran service until 1924, her final two seasons being with the 'tartan lum'. She was scrapped in 1925 at Port Glasgow by Smith & Co., but her name was perpetuated in the 1925 turbine and the popular 1957 car ferry. At almost 20 knots she must have been a superb sight.

Opposite: Glen Sannox (1892) at speed off Mount Stuart on a VIP cruise in her initial season.

Duchess of Rothesay (1895)

Duchess of Rothesay was built for the Caledonian Steam Packet in 1895 by J. & G. Thomson of Clydebank and was by far the best looking CSP paddler of all time. She had her promenade deck extended to the bow and open underneath to allow rope handling, like her predecessor *Duchess of Hamilton*.

After initially serving the Arran and Rothesay routes, she settled into the run to Arran via the Kyles, where she replaced *Ivanhoe* after 1897, and was popular and fast. In 1909 she was replaced by *Duchess of Hamilton* on the run to Arran via the Kyles and resumed running to Rothesay. In the peak seasons of 1911 and 1914 she was second steamer on the Ardrossan to Arran run to the turbine *Duchess of Argyll*. In pre-1914 days she was known as the 'cock of the walk' and carried a small weathercock at the top of her mast. She carried royalty in the persons of the Duke and Duchess of York, later King Edward VII and Queen Alexandra, to the opening of Cessnock Dock in Govan in September 1897, the Prince and Princess of Wales to the opening of Rothesay Dock in Clydebank in 1907 and the same couple, now King George V and Queen Mary, to visit the battleship HMS *Ramillies,* then under construction at the Beardmore yard at Dalmuir, in 1914.

Duchess of Rothesay was on the Wemyss Bay to Rothesay run in 1915 after the boom had been erected from the Cloch to Dunoon and was called up in late 1915 for service as the minesweeper HMS *Duke of Rothesay* in the Thames Estuary. As such she towed a downed Zeppelin into Margate, assisted in the salving of fourteen ships and swept up over 500 mines. Following her return from the war, she sank at her moorings at Merklands Wharf on 1 June 1919. Although many accounts state that this was because the sea cocks had been left open, it was actually because her mooring ropes were not slack enough to allow for the falling tide and she canted over and filled with water. She was raised by means of a coffer dam and refurbished and entered service again at the end of March 1920.

From then she was on the Princes Pier–Gourock–Rothesay–Tighnabruaich service, overnighting at Rothesay and making a morning sailing up to Gourock, a couple of early evening commuter runs to Dunoon, and an evening sailing down to Rothesay. In summer 1939 she returned to the haunts of her youth, running to Arran via the Kyles on certain days of the week.

She served her country again during the Second World War, initially as a minesweeper on the Clyde and at Dover and from April 1942 as an accommodation ship at Brightlingsea, on the River Colne in Essex. She was not fit for further duty at the end of the war and was towed to N.V. Machinehandel en Scheepslooperij 'De Koophandel', Nieuwe Lekkerland, Holland, for scrapping in 1946.

She was a ship of beauty and majesty and a flyer.

Opposite: Duchess of Rothesay (1895) in 1925 or later off Dunoon.

Jupiter (1896)

Jupiter was built in 1896 by J. & G. Thomson at Clydebank for the Glasgow & South Western Railway. From the outset she was of handsome profile and fast, making a mean speed of 18.18 knots on trials. She had compound diagonal engines and her promenade deck was extended to the bow and plated in below that, but the bridge was still in the traditional position aft of the funnel. She was based at Greenock Princes Pier, a pier and building of ornate Italianate style. *Jupiter* worked the run to Arran via the Kyles, competing in her first season with *Ivanhoe*, and then with *Duchess of Rothesay* in most summers until 1914. The 1901 schedule for the run to Arran via the Kyles called at Kirn, Dunoon, Innellan, Craigmore, Rothesay, Colintraive, Tighnabruaich, Corrie (a ferry call), Brodick, Lamlash, Kings Cross (another ferry call) and Whiting Bay. She left Princes Pier at 08:30 and arrived at Whiting Bay at 13:20, departing for the return sailing at 14:00 and sailing back direct from Corrie to Rothesay via Garroch Head, arriving back at Princes Pier at 17:30, with the return sailing being 45 minutes later on Saturdays. Following the pooling arrangement of 1908 with the CSP, she was only on the Arran via the Kyles service in that year, 1910 and 1914. In 1909, and from 1911 to 1913, she was on excursion service from Princes Pier and Fairlie.

Jupiter served as the minesweeper HMS *Jupiter II* from 1915 until 1920, serving as a minesweeper based at Dover. She returned to service in 1920 with a varied programme of cruises, running round the Lochs and Firth of Clyde on Mondays and Wednesdays, from Greenock to Ayr on Tuesdays and Thursdays, round Ailsa Craig on certain Fridays, with an afternoon trip to Tighnabruaich on Saturdays and a cruise round Bute on certain Sundays.

Following the railway amalgamation in 1923, she sailed in that summer with her GSWR grey hull and a yellow funnel with a black top and deep red band. In 1924 she had a black hull and the red band was very thin, and from 1926 she sailed with the familiar CSP livery of a yellow, black-topped funnel. She continued on excursion sailings until the arrival of *Caledonia* and *Mercury* in 1934, when she was placed on the Wemyss Bay to Millport service for her final two seasons until she was sold for breaking up at Barrow-in-Furness in 1935.

Her name continued with the 1937 paddle steamer (see below) and the 1973 car ferry. The 1896 paddler is ranked high in Clyde steamer history, as her 39 years in service testify.

Opposite: Jupiter (1896) off Tighnabruaich.

Waverley (1899)

By far one of the most outstanding steamers of the North British, *Waverley* was built in 1899 by A. & J. Inglis at Pointhouse and launched on 29 May of that year. She was the first NB steamer to be built for excursions and not railway connection services and had compound machinery, the first NB steamer to be built with such machinery, all previous ones having being built with single crank engines, and a haystack boiler. She was the first NB steamer to have saloons the full width of the hull and was a very fast steamer, making 19.73 knots on trials.

She was altered from having an open bow to a promenade deck extended to the bow for service in the 1914–18 war, an alteration retained on her return from war service. She was requisitioned for war service in November 1915 and served as a minesweeper until April 1919, on the east coast of England in the main, but also on the South Coast and in Belgian waters. Her refit after war service took until mid-1920 and her bridge was moved forward of the funnel at that time. She was fitted with a new boiler and a navy cowl to her funnel, which was removed after a couple of years.

She covered all the NB excursion routes, but with the winding up of the NBSP in 1902 and the transfer to direct railway ownership, she was restricted to up-Firth services, mainly sailing round Bute prior to the 1914 war, as the railway company was prohibited from sailing to Kintyre, Loch Fyne and the west of Arran. She was based at Craigendoran post-1920 and maintained the Lochgoilhead and Arrochar service with morning and evening runs to Rothesay. In 1932, in keeping with *Jeanie Deans*, she received an observation saloon, with a semi-circular front, forward on the promenade deck, similar to that on the present *Waverley*, and a new shelter aft on that deck. In 1936, in keeping with the remainder of the LNER fleet, her hull was painted grey. She was laid up in Bowling Harbour after the 1938 season and did not sail in scheduled service in 1939, although she was used to take evacuees to the coast in September, and following that duty, she was taken up by the Admiralty and her trendy grey hull became naval grey.

She was sunk at Dunkirk on 29 May 1940 after her rudder was damaged by a bomb. The story of her wartime exploits has often been told and will be as long as the 1947 *Waverley* continues in operation. With the closure of the Dunkirk Veterans Association some time ago, as age and infirmity take their toll and that generation of veterans passes on, it is now left to a different generation to tell the hell of Dunkirk and the steamers and men who did their bit for our freedom.

Opposite: *Waverley* (1899) between 1920, when her promenade deck was extended to the bow, and 1932, after which she received an observation saloon forwards, in Loch Goil.

Duchess of Fife (1903)

Duchess of Fife was built in 1903 at the Fairfield yard at Govan for the Caledonian Steam Packet Co. Ltd. She was an almost exact copy of *Duchess of Montrose*, built in the previous year by John Brown at Clydebank, although with larger paddle boxes and a raked funnel rather than the vertical one of the *Montrose*. It has always been a mystery why the order for *Duchess of Fife* went to Govan, but it may have been due to pressure of work at the Clydebank yard. She had two-crank, four-cylinder tandem triple expansion machinery and two navy boilers.

She joined the other titled ladies at Gourock and was very versatile, venturing on most of the CSP routes. She saw service in both wars, serving out of Grimsby and Dover as the minesweeper HMS *Duchess* from May 1916 to April 1919 and then from the outbreak of war in 1939 was an auxiliary minesweeper based at Harwich and took part in the Dunkirk evacuation, where she made three trips to the beaches and rescued 1,801 men. From 1941 to 1945 she was a training ship for minesweeping personnel based at Port Edgar on the Forth, and later on the Solent.

In 1923 and 1924 she adopted the 'tartan lum' with a thin red band below a black top, but in 1925 the yellow funnel with black top, familiar in the CSP fleet until 1972, was adopted.

Duchess of Fife saw much winter service, when her open bow on the main deck was winter-boarded, giving the effect at first glance of the more modern steamers which were plated to the bow.

In 1937 she grounded off Kirn, but had little damage and from 1937 onwards she moved from general railway connection work from Gourock and Wemyss Bay to the Wemyss Bay to Millport and Kilchattan Bay service.

Immediately after the Second World War she was given a major rebuild at Port Glasgow and, in common with the remainder of the CSP fleet, received a wheelhouse in 1948. In service she was seen on the Holy Loch, and Millport and Kilchattan Bay routes until her illustrious career closed in June 1953 at the age of 50, by which time she was the last surviving pre-1914 steamer on the Firth. She was rendered redundant by the new building programme of the *ABC* car ferries and the four *Maids*.

Opposite: Duchess of Fife (1903) arriving at Dunoon in 1923 with the 'tartan lum'.

Prince Edward (1911)

Launched in 1911 at the yard of A. & J. Inglis at Pointhouse, the masters of Clyde steamer design and style, it took until July 1912 for the *Prince Edward* to reach Loch Lomond, missing the tide on the River Leven and being almost aground at Kirkland on 4 May 1911. It was not until 4 November that the water in the river was high enough to float her and for her to progress to Balloch, at one point reportedly enlisting the help of a class of local schoolchildren to weigh her down enough to clear the bridge at Alexandria/Bonhill. *Maid of the Loch* did not attempt the trip up the Leven and was prefabricated and assembled at Balloch after the various parts had been taken there by train.

She was the largest steamer on the loch, having compound diagonal machinery. She ran as part of a twice daily service on the traditional route criss-crossing the loch from Balloch to Balmaha, Luss, Rowadennan, Tarbet, Inversnaid and Ardlui, running alongside *Empress* of 1888 until her withdrawal in 1925, sisters *Prince George* and *Princess May* of 1898 until their withdrawal from regular service in 1936 and 1953 respectively, and *Maid of the Loch* until it was deemed in 1955 that there was not the traffic on the Loch for two steamers and she was withdrawn and scrapped. It is a great pity that she did not survive until the modern-day craze for Victorian and Edwardian design meant that she would have been an ideal candidate for preservation.

Opposite: Prince Edward (1911) off Balloch Pier in 1949–52 colours.

Queen Empress (1912)

Queen Empress, the final Clyde paddle steamer before the 1918 war, was built in 1912 by Murdoch & Murray of Port Glasgow with compound diagonal machinery by Rankine & Blackmore, similar to that installed in *Maid of the Loch* but larger, for John Williamson & Co. She maintained the Rothesay and Lochgoilhead routes from the Broomielaw, and was on the Campbeltown route for two weeks each September.

She served her country in both world wars, operating as a troopship from Southampton to the French ports and then as a minesweeper based on the Tyne during the 1914–18 conflict and was sent to the White Sea in 1919 as an ambulance transport to support White Russian forces. She did not have an easy time there, running aground at one point, and towing the Clyde turbine steamer *King Edward* off a shoal after the latter had run aground.

In the 1920s and 1930s she offered a variety of long distance excursions on the Firth, mainly to Ayr, Inveraray, Campbeltown, all from Helensburgh and piers to Millport, and to the east Arran piers, Girvan and round Ailsa Craig from Dunoon, Largs and Millport. From 1936 she was on railway connection services from Greenock, Gourock and Wemyss Bay.

From 1935 to spring 1936 she was under the ownership of the Caledonian Steam Packet, and then by Williamson-Buchanan Steamers (1936) Ltd, and from March 1938 by the London, Midland & Scottish Railway until transferred to the CSP in 1943. From 1938 she was in CSP livery.

From 1940 she was the flagship of the 12th Minesweeper Flotilla and was sold after completion of war service on 9 August 1946 to N.V. Machinehandel en Scheepslooperij 'De Koophandel', Nieuwe Lekkerland, Holland, for scrapping.

Opposite: Queen Empress (1912) between 1920 and 1924 leaving Dunoon.

Jeanie Deans (1931)

Built in 1931 at the Fairfield yard at Govan for the London & North Eastern Railway for service from Craigendoran, *Jeanie Deans* had the first triple expansion three-crank engine on a steamer built for Clyde service. She was very fast and capable of doing long distance excursions. She had an observation saloon forward on the promenade deck added in 1932. Her funnels were originally very short and the forward funnel was lengthened by 9 feet prior to the 1932 season, giving her an unbalanced appearance for the remainder of that decade. From 1936 until 1939 she was painted in the grey hull colour scheme, as were the other LNER steamers, in an attempt to make them look more modern.

In the pre-war years her route was to Lochgoilhead and Arrochar, including morning and evening sailings to Rothesay. There were also some long-distance sailings, including ones to Ayr and round Ailsa Craig on Tuesdays and Thursdays from 1932 until 1937.

During the war years she served as a minesweeper, as flagship of the 11th Minesweeping Flotilla, based on the Clyde, and later at Portsmouth and Milford Haven, from September 1939 until March 1941, from which time she was used as an anti-aircraft ship on the Thames until 1945.

In 1946, following war service, she was rebuilt using the 1939 drawings of the present *Waverley* at A. & J. Inglis' yard at Pointhouse and re-entered service looking very handsome in May 1946. On Nationalisation in 1948 she came under the ownership of the British Transport Commission and received the Caledonian Steam Packet black-topped yellow funnel, being transferred to the ownership of the latter in 1953. From 1948 until the mid-1950s her dining saloon windows were in two-inch black wood, but were removed and painted white along with the remainder of the superstructure.

Her main route in post-war years was the Round Bute cruise on weekdays, with a morning return to Rothesay, and an afternoon trip on Saturdays to Tighnabruaich and Sunday excursions to off Skipness. In her latter years she alternated with *Waverley*, running in alternate weeks to Arran via the Kyles of Bute on Mondays, Lochgoilhead and Arrochar on Tuesdays and Thursdays, Round the Lochs and Firth of Clyde on Wednesdays, and Craigendoran to Rothesay sailings on Saturdays, occasionally doing the up-river cruise from Largs to Bridge Wharf on Fridays.

Jeanie was withdrawn after the 1964 season and sold for use on the Thames, where she was renamed *Queen of the South* and regained the red, white and black funnels of the LNER era. Her owner, Mr Don Rose, formed the Coastal Steam Packet Co. Ltd in 1965, but sadly the venture only survived for a short period with little in the way of any credible operation. She was sold for breaking up in Belgium, at Boom near Antwerp, in 1967. A visit to the breakers yard some dozen years later by one of the authors found a derelict site with postcards of her as *Queen of the South* blowing in the wind.

Jeanie was a very special steamer, large and fast, and her name resonates in the heart and minds of all with whom she made contact. Round Bute on the *Jeanie* is still remembered fondly today, nearly fifty years since she left the Firth.

Opposite: Jeanie Deans (1931) off Rothesay in 1948 with the dark saloon window frames.

Caledonia (1934)/HMS Goatfell 1939–45

Built by William Denny of Dumbarton in 1934 for the Caledonian Steam Packet Co. Ltd, as a sister of the Fairfield-built *Mercury*, which was a war loss, *Caledonia* was fitted with triple expansion machinery and remained in service until October 1969. She was of an unusual design, with an upper deck above the observation saloon connected to the deck above the aft deckhouse with hinged walkways, which could be raised when she was used to carry vehicles. She had disguised paddle boxes, claimed to be intended to make her look like a turbine steamer from a distance.

When built she was used on rail-connected services including that from Wemyss Bay to Rothesay and the Kyles of Bute and was also on a Gourock to Ormidale service. From 1935 to 1938 she was on the run from Gourock to Arran via the Kyles of Bute and in 1939 alternated weekly with *Mercury* between that run and sailings from Wemyss Bay to Rothesay and the Kyles of Bute piers.

In late 1939 she was requisitioned for war service and served as the minesweeper HMS *Goatfell*, latterly serving as a patrol vessel. She was present at D-Day and sailed to open navigation to Antwerp in late 1945.

On reconditioning after war service she was placed on the Gourock to Rothesay run and, from 1954, became the Ayr excursion steamer, with a wide variety of destinations. In 1964, for example, she sailed on Sundays alternately to Rothesay and Loch Riddon and to Dunoon and Loch Goil, Mondays to Brodick and Campbeltown, Tuesdays to Millport, Dunoon and a cruise to Loch Goil alternating with Rothesay and Tighnabruaich, Wednesdays an afternoon cruise to Brodick or Millport, and Thursdays to Brodick and Rothesay or Dunoon. All sailings were also offered from Troon. On Fridays she occasionally deputised for *Waverley* on the up-river cruise from Largs to Glasgow and was used as a back-up steamer on Saturdays on the main point-to-point services from Ardrossan to Brodick or Wemyss Bay to Rothesay. In 1965 she was transferred to Craigendoran to replace *Jeanie Deans* and from then until her withdrawal in 1969, she operated on a variety of excursion sailings from the north bank pier.

She was held in high regard and was the first PSPS candidate for preservation in 1970, which would have seen her based at Oban if successful.

She was purchased by Bass Charrington and became the floating pub *Old Caledonia* on the Thames at Hungerford Bridge in the centre of London until destroyed by fire on 27 April 1980.

Opposite: *Caledonia* (1934) at Gourock in May 1968, dressed overall for a CRSC charter.

Jupiter (1937)/HMS Scawfell 1939–45

Built by Fairfield in Govan for the Caledonian Steam Packet in 1937, *Jupiter* was a sister of *Juno*, which was a war loss, and had three-crank triple expansion machinery and a double-ended boiler with two funnels. She was built for ferry services and short cruises. During her 20-year lifetime, she maintained service up-firth and relieved at Ayr and on the Arran and Holy Loch runs.

Called up for war service in late 1939, she was renamed HMS *Scawfell* and served as a minesweeper as part of the 11th Minesweeping Flotilla, based initially at Milford Haven and later at Dover. She later became an escort ship, making some trips to Holland, and serving between the Tyne and the Humber. She was then an anti-aircraft defence ship on the Thames and took part in the D-Day landings in Normandy in June 1944, bringing down three enemy aircraft.

She was the first Clyde steamer to resume service after the war, being refitted at the A. & J. Inglis yard at Pointhouse, and entered service in February 1946 on the Holy Loch route. Her main service in post-war years was from Gourock and Wemyss Bay to Rothesay. She was converted to oil-firing in the winter of 1956/57 and offered Sunday afternoon cruises from Bridge Wharf to Lochgoilhead in the 1957 season, but was really surplus to requirements after the introduction of the ABC car ferries and the four *Maids* in 1953–54. She was withdrawn after the 1957 season and was laid up in the Albert Harbour, Greenock, leaving the Clyde for scrapping in Dublin in April 1961. Plans to sell her to Cosens of Weymouth for work on the South Coast to replace their aging *Consul* (1896), *Monarch* (1924), ex-*Shanklin*, and *Embassy* (1911) had fallen through.

Opposite: Jupiter (1937) in her inaugural season of 1937.

Waverley (1947) at Craigendoran in the mid-1960s.

Waverley (1947)

Waverley was built at A. & J. Inglis' Pointhouse yard at the mouth of the River Kelvin. She was originally designed in 1938 but building was put on hold because of the war. Her plans were used extensively in the January–May 1946 rebuild of *Jeanie Deans* at Pointhouse. Her first season in 1947 was delayed due to the severe winter, which saw the longest cold snap in years. *Waverley*'s maiden voyage reopened the popular Three Lochs Tour and reopened Lochgoilhead and Arrochar piers, closed since the outbreak of war in 1939. 16 June 1947 saw the last ever Clyde steamer enter service, the only Clyde paddler to adopt a raked bow and the largest ever triple expansion engine to be fitted to a Clyde steamer.

In 1948 she adopted yellow and black funnels in line with the remainder of the former LNER fleet at the time of nationalisation. She operated above the Cumbraes on Clyde services from 1947 to 1951 and was used extensively on longer excursions from 1951 to 1972, including Ayr, Inveraray, and Campbeltown. She became the last sea-going paddle steamer in Europe in 1970 and the last sea-going paddle steamer in the world in 1975.

She made the last ever call at Innellan in 1972 and, as the final Clyde paddle steamer in service, used all open piers in the final year of the CSP in 1972 and in 1973 in CalMac colours. During her years in preservation since 1975, she has utilised all surviving Clyde piers, including unique calls at Portencross, Carradale and Otter Ferry; although calls at the remains of Craigendoran, Arrochar and the old pier at Lochranza were scheduled on enthusiast charters, they were never called at. A new pier was opened for use by her at Lochranza in 2003 and Blairmore pier was restored and re-opened for her in 2004.

In 1973 the Scottish Transport Group/Caledonian MacBrayne under Sir Patrick Thomas, Maurice Little and John Whittle made the offer of a lifetime, 'A pound and she's yours', to the Paddle Steamer Preservation Society. Waverley Steam Navigation Co. Ltd was formed as the new owners and has continued to own her to date.

The contribution of the following must be acknowledged in aiding *Waverley* through difficult and challenging times to give the British public rare and delightful opportunities of going to sea in a paddle steamer: Captain D. L. Neill (Master, 1975–97), Terry Sylvester, David Duncanson, Ian Muir, Ken Blacklock and the many and countless others who have sailed as crew on the steamer and have participated in winter work parties, but these gentlemen knew the business and gave their all to it.

During *Waverley*'s 37 years in preservation she has steamed round the UK six times, three on a UK tour, sailed off the French coast in 1980 and 1990 to celebrate the 40th and 50th anniversaries of the Dunkirk evacuation, taken part in the D-Day commemorations in 1994 marking 50 years, and has sailed in the wake of many long since gone paddle steamers on anniversary excursions since 1975. Many heart stopping moments have not been recorded here but she has continued to steam for over 37 years in preservation, ten more than in her earlier existence. Her 65-year history on the Firth has only been surpassed by the 1864 *Iona* and the 1846 *Mary Jane/Glencoe*.

This book was launched aboard *Waverley* in August 2012 on a cruise to mark the bicentenary of the paddle steamer *Comet*. Sadly *Waverley* will be the last ever but let us all hope as 'Friends of the Waverley' that she continues to ply the Firth for many more years in the wake of the *Comet*.

Maid of the Loch (1953) arriving at Ardlui in the 1960s.

Maid of the Loch (1953)

Maid of the Loch was the final paddle steamer to be built for Loch Lomond and was built by A. & J. Inglis at Pointhouse in sections and assembled on the slipway at Balloch. While being assembled she had a yellow funnel with a black top, but by the time of her launch this was yellow overall.

Various plans for the steamers on Loch Lomond had been mooted, including reboiling *Prince Edward* with no new vessel being built and transferring *Marchioness of Lorne* from the Firth to the Loch, although it was found that she would have been too deep-draughted for the loch piers. Hence the *Maid* was built. The *Maid* title came on the back of the four new Clyde motorships, although the plan originally was to name her *Princess Anne*.

She was built in grand style and few would dispute her worth in the vagaries of the Scottish weather, but few would argue that she was too big and rather unwieldy and she did much to destroy the loch piers during spells of windy weather. Her all-white livery made much of the dark corners of the loch. She had many good points, including her shelter deck, the paddle box stairwells, a traditional feature of Loch Lomond steamers, and her big roomy saloons.

She normally made two rounds of the loch from Balloch to Ardlui in the height of the season and Wednesday showboat cruises. She made connections at Tarbert with the Three Lochs Tour involving *Waverley* or *Jeanie Deans* and at Inversnaid with the Trossachs Tour involving the screw steamer *Sir Walter Scott* on Loch Katrine.

The closure of Balmaha Pier in 1963, Ardlui in 1967 and Tarbet in 1974 left her only able to call at Rowardennan and Inversnaid. Luss Pier, which had been closed prior to her entry into service, re-opened in 1980. Inversnaid, as mentioned above, allowed for connections to Loch Katrine, and Rowardennan to the ascent of Ben Lomond. Both allowed access to the West Highland Way after the latter was established in 1980, although a path between the two piers was in existence much earlier.

In 1975 she briefly had a yellow and black funnel at the start of the season, then briefly a yellow, red and black one, quickly changed to a red black-topped funnel, but 1976 saw a return to the all-yellow funnel.

Her final season in 1981 brought to a close many years of uncertainty, with reports of her proposed withdrawal having appeared as early as 1961. It is unlikely that her operation ever made much money for her owners, losses being recorded of £6,000 in 1966, and £7,000 in 1967, rising to £73,450 in her final season of 1981. The closure of Arrochar pier in 1972 and the cessation of the Three Lochs Tour was a major blow to passenger numbers.

The fight for her to return to service has continued for longer than she was in service and she is now under the aegis of the Loch Lomond Steamship Company, which continues to search for avenues to bring her into steam again. She has been fully restored internally and is an ideal venue for weddings and functions. The adjacent steam-powered winch house and slipway is now fully operational and forms the ideal based for a hopeful return to service and for refits and repairs.

She is currently in the livery of a black hull, white superstructure and red funnel with a black top. The engine had been restored so it can be moved manually. Much of her equipment was removed or stolen over the years and her wheelhouse is more or less empty, with no wheel or telegraph or other navigational equipment. Her boiler was removed at an early stage of internal restoration. The replacement of the boiler and the wheelhouse equipment will be required if she is to steam again and as this book goes to press, a public appeal is being launched to raise money for this, so that she can steam in 2013 and return to service in 2014. The establishment of the Loch Lomond and the Trossachs National Park on 2002 has meant a higher profile for the loch and the possibility of funding to enable a return to steam for the *Maid* and of higher publicity for her once she has returned to service. Rebuilding of piers at Balmaha, Tarbet and Ardlui would be essential for a return to the traditional service and the rebuilding of Arrochar Pier to the re-introduction of the Three Lochs Tour.

Comet replica (1962)

So far our previous twenty steamers have concentrated on the classics, many of these built by J. & G. Thomson at Clydebank, but for number twenty-one we had to return to *Comet* of 1962, for she fully deserves to be the last Clyde paddler ever built and brings our story to a conclusion.

Her hull was built at Buckie by the yard of George Thomson, builders of wooden fishing boats, as a full-size replica of Henry Bell's 1812 *Comet*. She was fitted out at Lithgows yard at Port Glasgow, near to John Wood's yard, where the original was built, Lithgows having built the engine as a special project by their apprentices.She was launched and steamed the same day; among the small craft in attendance was a CSP *Maid* and *Queen Mary II* steamed past.

The 150th Anniversary *Comet* visited Greenock, Helensburgh and Glasgow Bridge Wharf, all in steam, and carrying VIP passengers from Greenock to Helensburgh on 1 September 1962, in her short tour of duty. She spent some time in a shed at Port Glasgow and was then given a dry land berth in the centre of Port Glasgow. Two major overhauls have seem her visit Irvine and Ferguson's yard at Port Glasgow, all by road, and she has also visited Helensburgh on the back of a low loader, crossing the Erskine Bridge in the process. She can thus claim to be the only Clyde paddle steamer to visit a shipyard by the back door, with no water under her keel.

It is fitting that we close with her as in 2012 both authors fully acknowledge the apprentices of Lithgows Ltd who built her as a true memorial to the introduction of steam to European waters.

In 1812 came the reality of Henry Bell's vision and in 1912 a full centenary review was held on the Clyde with examples of the nation's ships on display at the Tail of the Bank.

In 1962 the replica, in full steam, re-enacted history on the river.

In 2012 the only tangible acknowledgement is PS *Waverley* on 10 August on an ordinary day out celebrating, or is it a sad reflection on how our history, 200 years of steam navigation in Europe, features little in the mind of people today?

Somehow the Clyde River and Firth has become the *Waverley* and her alone. Hopefully this publication puts it all in context, but if you pass through Port Glasgow look for the paddle steamer *Comet* on its plinth and spare a thought for Henry Bell, the man who put steam on the Clyde and so gave birth to a new and wonderful age that spread throughout the United Kingdom, to Europe and the World with paddle propulsion and steam power.

A monument at Helensburgh and another at Dunglass fully acknowledges Bell and his vision. A commemorative plaque was placed near to Wood's yard in Port Glasgow in 1973, but its whereabouts today is unknown.

Waverley on 10 August 2012 launched this book, 200 years to the day from the maiden voyage of *Comet* from Glasgow to Greenock, the first paddle steamer in Europe, and whose replica was the last paddle steamer built for the Clyde or West Highlands.

Opposite: The 1962 *Comet* replica on her plinth at Port Glasgow, complete with Christmas decorations, in the late 1970s.

Bibliography

Clyde & West Highlands

Bowman, A. I.: *Swifts & Queens: Passenger Transport on the Forth & Clyde Canal*: Strathkelvin District Libraries & Museums, Bishopbriggs: 1984

Brown, Alan: *Loch Lomond Passenger Steamers 1818–1989*: Allan T. Condie Publications: 2000

Brown, Alan: *Craigendoran Steamers*: Waverley Excursions Ltd., Glasgow: 3rd Edition: 2007

Brown, Alan & Polglaze, Richard: *HMS Aristocrat: a Paddler at War*: Waverley Excursions Ltd, Glasgow, 1995

Campbell, Colin & Fenton, Roy: *Ships in Focus: Burns and Laird*: Ships in Focus Publications, Preston: 1999

Clyde River Steamer Club: various publications including
Services to Inveraray and Upper Loch Fyne –cruise brochure 4 May 1968
The Arrochar Route –cruise brochure 7 September 1968
The East Arran Piers from the upper Firth – cruise brochure 23 September 1967
The Royal Route –cruise brochure 5 September 1970
The Campbeltown Route: Ian McCrorie –cruise brochure 6 May 1972
The Gareloch Route: Ian McCrorie – cruise brochure from 16 September 1972
The Millport Route: Ian McCrorie –cruise brochure 4 May 1974
Various issues of *Clyde Steamers Magazine*: 1967 to date

Davidson, A. S.: *Marine Art and the Clyde; 100 Years of Sea, Sail and Steam*: Jones-Sands Publishing, Upton, Wirral: 2001

Davies, Kenneth: *The Clyde Passenger Steamers*: Kyle Publications Ltd, Ayr: 1980 (has many inaccuracies)

Duckworth, C. L. D. & Langmuir, G. E.: *Clyde River and other Steamers*: 4th edition; Brown, Son and Ferguson Ltd, Glasgow: 1990

Duckworth, C. L. D. & Langmuir, G. E.: *West Highland Steamers*: 4th edition; Brown, Son and Ferguson Ltd, Glasgow: 1987

Duckworth, C. L. D. & Langmuir, G. E.: *Clyde and other Coastal Steamers*: 2nd edition; T. Stephenson & Sons Ltd, Prescot, Lancashire: 1977

Duckworth, C. L. D. & Langmuir, G. E.: *Railway and other Steamers*: 2nd edition; T. Stephenson & Sons Ltd, Prescot, Lancashire: 1968

Harvey, W. J. & Telford, P. J.: *The Clyde Shipping Company, Glasgow: 1815–2000*: P. J. Telford: 2002

Hawks, F. W.: *British 19th Century Steamships: Issue 4 Steamers to 1840* (CD): World Ship Society 2012

Hope, Iain: *The Campbells of Kilmun*: Aggregate Publications, Johnstone; 1981

Lyon, David J.: *Part I & Part IV: The Denny List*: National Maritime Museum, London: 1975–1976

MacArthur, Iain C.: *The Caledonian Steam Packet Co. Ltd*: The Clyde River Steamer Club, Glasgow: 1971

David MacBrayne Ltd: *MacBrayne Centenary: One Hundred Years of Progress 1851–1951*: David MacBrayne Ltd., Glasgow 1951

McCrorie, Ian: *Clyde Pleasure Steamers; an Illustrated History*: Orr, Pollock & Co., Greenock: 1986

MacHaffie, Fraser G.: *The Short Sea Route*: T. Stephenson & Sons Ltd, Prescot, Lancashire: 1975

McQueen, Andrew: *Clyde River-Steamers of the Past Fifty Years*: Gowans and Gray Ltd, Glasgow and London: 1923

McQueen, Andrew: *Echoes of Old Clyde Paddle-Wheels*: Gowans and Gray Ltd, Glasgow and London: 1924

Moir, Peter and Crawford, Ian: *Clyde Shipwrecks*: MoirCrawford, Wemyss Bay, 1988

Moir, Peter and Crawford, Ian: *Argyll Shipwrecks*: Moir Crawford, Wemyss Bay, 1994

David Napier, Engineer 1790-1869: An Autobiographical sketch with notes: James MacLehose & Sons, Glasgow: 1912

Osborne, Brian: *The Ingenious Mr Bell*: Argyll Publishing, Glendaruel: 1995

Osborne, J. Craig (Comp.): *The Comet and her Creators: The Men Who Built PS Comet and Her Career*: J Craig Osborne: 2007

Paterson, Alan J. S.: *The Victorian Summer of the Clyde Steamers (1864–1888)*: David & Charles, Newton Abbot: 1972

Paterson, Alan J. S.: *The Golden Years of the Clyde Steamers (1889–1914)*: David & Charles, Newton Abbot: 1969

Paterson, Alan J. S.: *Classic Scottish Paddle Steamers*: David & Charles, Newton Abbot: 1982

Plummer, Russell (compiled and edited by): *Paddle Steamers at War 1939–1945*: GMS Enterprises, Peterborough: 1995

Plummer, Russell: *The Ships that Saved an Army: A comprehensive record of the 1,300 'Little Ships' of Dunkirk*: Patrick Stephens Ltd, 1990

Robertson, R. G.; 'Clyde Paddle Steamers at War'; in *Ships Monthly* Vol. 1, Nos 8 & 9

Robins, Nick: *Passenger Tugs and Tenders*: Bernard McCall, Portishead: 2010

Smart, Iain: *The Lochgoil and Lochlong Steamboat Company*: Lochgoil Publishing, Lochgoilhead 2008

Somerville, Cameron: *Colour on the Clyde*: Bute Newspapers Ltd., Rothesay: n.d. (1970)

The Comet Trust, Port Glasgow: *The Story of Henry Bell's Comet*: n.d. (1962–3)

Thomas, John: *British Railways Steamers of the Clyde*: Ian Allan Ltd, London: 1948

Thomas, John: *A Regional History of the Railways of Great Britain: Volume 6: Scotland, the Lowlands and the Borders*: David & Charles, Newton Abbot: 1971

Thomas, P. N.: *Steamships 1835–1875 in contemporary records* (with CD): Waine Research Publications, Wolverhampton, N.D. (2008) (CD is useful but owner is often listed as the representative of the owners who registered the ship rather than the owner's name)

Watson, Donald: *From Comet to Caledonia*: Brown, Son & Ferguson Ltd., Glasgow: 1999

Williamson, Capt James: *The Clyde Passenger Steamer, its Rise and Progress during the Nineteenth Century From the 'Comet' of 1812 to the 'King Edward' of 1901*: James MacLehose and Son, Glasgow: 1904

Walker, Fred M.: *Song of the Clyde; a History of Clyde Shipbuilding*: Patrick Stephens Ltd. Cambridge: 1984

Wilson, Roy: *Passenger Steamers of the Glasgow & South Western Railway*: Twelveheads Press, Truro: 1991

Winser, John de S: *B.E.F.Ships before, at and after Dunkirk*: World Ship Society, Gravesend: 1999

The Clyde-built ship list on www.clydesite.co.uk

East Coast of Scotland

Brodie, Ian: *Steamers of the Forth*: David & Charles, Newton Abbot: 1976

Brodie, Ian: *Steamers of the Tay*: Stenlake Publishing: 2003

England Wales & Ireland

Burtt, Frank: *Cross Channel and Coastal Paddle Steamers*: Richard Tilling, London 1934

Burtt, Frank: *Steamers of the Thames and Medway*: Richard Tilling, London 1949

Clammer, Richard: *Cosens of Weymouth: 1848–1918: A History of the Bournemouth, Weymouth and Swanage Paddle Steamers*: Black Dwarf Publications Witney, Oxon & Lydney, Glos: 2005

Cowell, John: *Liverpool to North Wales Pleasure Steamers: A Pictorial History: 1821–1962*: S. B. Publications, Market Drayton: 1990

Duckworth, C. L. D. & Langmuir, G. E.: *West Coast Steamers*: 3rd edition; T. Stephenson & Sons Ltd, Prescot, Lancashire: 1966

Easdown, Martin & Sage, Linda: *Piers of Hampshire and the Isle of Wight*: Amberley Publishing, Stroud, Glos: 2011

Farr, Grahame: *West Country Pleasure Steamers*: 2nd edition: T. Stephenson & Sons Ltd, Prescot, Lancashire: 1967

Grasemann, C. & McLachlan, G. W. P.: *English Channel Packet Boats*: Syren & Shipping Ltd, London 1939

Handley, Chris: *Maritime Activities of the Somerset and Dorset Railway*: Millstream Books, Bath: 2001

Kittridge, Alan: *Steamers and Ferries of Cornwall and the Isles of Scilly*: Tempus Publishing, Stroud: 2004

McNeill, D. B.: *Irish Passenger Steamship Services: Volume 1: North of Ireland*: David & Charles, Newton Abbot: 1969

McNeill, D. B.: *Irish Passenger Steamship Services: Volume 2: South of Ireland*: David & Charles, Newton Abbot: 1971

Mayne, Richard: *Mail Ships of the Channel Islands*: Picton Publishing, Chippenham: 1971

Maund, T. B.: *Mersey Ferries, Volume 1 - Woodside to Eastham*: Transport Publishing Co., Glossop: 1991

Maund, T. B. & Jenkins, Martin: *Mersey Ferries: Volume 2 – The Wallasey Ferries*: Black Dwarf Publications, Lydney, Glos: 2003

O'Brien, Captain F. T.: *Early Solent Steamers; a History of Local Steam Navigation*: David & Charles, Newton Abbot: 1973

Shepherd, John: *The Liverpool and North Wales Steamship Company*: Ships in Focus Publications, Preston: 2006

Sherwood, Tim: *The Steamboat Revolution; London's First Steamships*: Tempus Publishing, Stroud: 2007

Thornton, E. C. B.: *Steamers of North Wales*: 2nd Edition: T. Stephenson & Sons Ltd, Prescot, Lancashire: 1962

Thornton, E. C. B.: *South Coast Pleasure Steamers*: 2nd edition: T. Stephenson & Sons Ltd, Prescot, Lancashire: 1969

Wall, Robert: *Bristol Channel Pleasure Steamers*: David & Charles, Newton Abbot: 1973

Europe

Güleryüz, Ahmet: *Istanbul Vapurlari/Istanbul Ferries*: Demizler Kitabevi, Istanbul, Turkey: 2005

Jansson, Christer: *Med ÅngbåtfrånHelsiongborg; Passagerarfarten under 1800-talet*: Frank Stenvalls Förlag, Malmö: 1982

Pittelkow, Kurt &Schmelzkopf, Reinhart: *Heimathafen Stettin*: Strandgut, Cuxhafen: 1987

Thorsoe, Søren and others: *DFDS 1866–1991: Ship Development through 125 years from paddle steamers to RoRo ship*: DFDS & World Ship Society: 1991

Tutel, Eser: *Seyr-I Sefain, Oncesivesonrasi*: IletisimYayncilik, Istanbul: 1997

Tutel, Eser: *Gemiler ... Süvariler ... Iskeleler ...*: IletisimYayinlari, Istanbul: 1998

U S A & Canada

Ashdown, Dana: *Railway Steamships of Ontario*: The Boston Mills Press, Erin, Ontario, Canada: 1985

Graham, Eric J.: *Clyde Built Blockade Runners, Cruisers and Armoured Rams of the American Civil War*: Birlinn Ltd, Edinburgh: 2006

Wise, Stephen R.: *Lifeline of the Confederacy: Blockade Running during the Civil War*: University of South Carolina Press, Columbia, South Carolina, U S A: 1988

Australia and New Zealand

Parsons, Ronald: *Paddle Steamers of Australasia*: 3rd Edition: Ronald Parsons, Lobethal, S A, Australia: 1973

Plowman, Peter: *The Wheels Still Turn; A History of Australian Paddleboats*: Kangaroo Press, Kenthurst, Australia: 1992

Clyde Coast Piers

Alistair Deayton

The fascinating history of Scottish piers illustrated through a
wonderful collection of images.

978 1 84868 427 0